Informal Tests
for Diagnosing
Specific
Reading Problems

Informal Tests
for Diagnosing
Specific
Reading Problems

Stephen A. Pavlak, Ph.D.

Professor of Education
California University of Pennsylvania
California, Pennsylvania

Parker Publishing Company, Inc.
West Nyack, New York 10994

Library of Congress Cataloging in Publication Data

Pavlak, Stephen A.
    Informal tests for diagnosing specific reading
problems.

    1. Reading—Ability testing.   I. Title.
LB1050.46.P38   1984   372.4′076   84-19094

ISBN 0-13-464801-3

Printed in the United States of America

ABOUT THIS BOOK
OF DIAGNOSTIC READING AIDS

The purpose of this book is to give reading specialists and classroom teachers a store of ready-to-use informal diagnostic aids that can be easily adapted in any reading program. The aids included provide a quick, reliable way to identify and verify the various problems students have in reading in order to prescribe effective corrective or remedial activities for each individual.

The book presents scores of informal reading tests in the basic skill areas of phonic analysis, structural analysis, and comprehension for use with primary and intermediate level readers, as well as inventories in survival reading skills that will be particularly useful with students at the intermediate and upper levels. It also provides a simple recordkeeping device, the "Individual Pupil Checklist of Reading Skills," parent and child interview forms, and interest inventories and attitude surveys for both the primary and intermediate levels.

Note: All of these diagnostic and recordkeeping aids can be copied by the individual reading specialist or classroom teacher as many times as required for individual, group or whole-class use.

These evaluative tools are sequenced in the order in which they would generally be used. You can first administer the informal inventories and then analyze and record results on the Individual Pupil Checklist. After you have identified and recorded a pupil's skill deficiencies, you can focus on his or her interests and attitudes using the interview forms, interest inventories, and attitude surveys.

While all of the informal tests and other aids in this book will be useful tools in your diagnostic program, the "Individual Pupil Checklist of Reading Skills" will be of special value when used with the corrective activities presented in *Classroom Activities for Correcting Specific Reading Problems*, a separately printed book available from the publisher. The reinforcement activities, exercises and/or games in this book are keyed to the items on the Individual Pupil Checklist. The book thus provides a ready store of prescriptive activities you can use after you have evaluated a pupil's specific areas of weakness and recorded them on the Checklist.

I hope you find the diagnostic materials presented on the following pages valuable in helping each of your students learn to read to the extent of his or her ability.

Stephen A. Pavlak

ACKNOWLEDGMENTS

I am indebted to my wife Patricia for her encouragement, advice, and editorial skill. Without her help, this book would not have been possible. I would also like to acknowledge the support and inspiration of my parents and my children, Stephen and Nancy.

CONTENTS

SECTION 2
INDIVIDUAL PUPIL CHECKLIST OF READING SKILLS

SECTION 3
INTERVIEW FORMS

SECTION 4
INTEREST INVENTORIES

SECTION 5
ATTITUDE SURVEYS

Section 1

INFORMAL
READING
INVENTORIES

Four informal reading inventories, covering phonic analysis, structural analysis, comprehension skills, and survival reading skills, are presented in Section I. These four inventories are designed so that you can use them as diagnostic tools. Because the inventories list specific skill areas, they will provide you with diagnostic information that is keyed to specific reading skill areas. These inventories should not, however, be viewed as a battery of tests that must be given together. Rather, you may present each section of each inventory as an individual test. As you will see by reading the directions for each skill area, the inventories do not have to be administered as a total test. This will give you greater flexibility in using the inventories. You can use your own judgment in selecting which parts of the inventories to administer to your pupils.

Because the inventories are to be used as diagnostic instruments, they contain their own recordkeeping checklists. You can tabulate the results on each section of the inventory as your testing progresses, and record the results on the "Individual Pupil Checklist of Reading Skills." The checklists included with each inventory can be easily reproduced for use with each student.

INFORMAL PHONIC ANALYSIS INVENTORIES

TEACHER'S GUIDE

Introduction

The following informal reading inventories have been designed to evaluate specific tasks in the area of phonic analysis. No child is expected to complete the entire series. Some skills may be too advanced, others too easy. The number of skills tested is determined by the examiner. Administering the complete test takes approximately forty minutes.

When completing each subtest of the Informal Reading Inventories, a child's score is never compared with the score of another child in the room or in another area of the country. The only comparison made is between the child's PRETEST score and his or her POSTTEST score.

Directions

The following are general directions for administering the informal phonic analysis inventories. Specific directions for those tests to be administered orally are provided in the "Answer Key and Directions for the Phonic Analysis Inventories" on pages 25-29.

1. Decide which skills need to be measured and test only those skills.
2. Explain EXACTLY what the child is expected to do.
3. Administer each skill test separately.
4. Write any immediate comments before administering the next test.
5. Give the child a rest period when needed. Do not expect the student to complete too many tasks at one sitting.
6. When ** appear beside a test title on the student's test copy, you will need to turn to this test in the Answer Key and Directions, on pages 25-29. These tests are oral tests and the words to be read aloud are contained in the Answer Key and Directions.

Scoring

1. Refer to the Answer Key and Directions on pages 25-29 for the correct answers.
2. Use the "Conversion Table for Computing Percentage of Accuracy" in converting the number of items correct on each test to percentages. The percentages should be written in the accuracy blank on each test.

CONVERSION TABLE FOR COMPUTING PERCENTAGE OF ACCURACY

POSSIBLE RIGHT ANSWERS ————————————————————→

	10	11	12	13	14	15	16	17	18	19	20	21	22	23	24	25	26
1.	10	9	8	8	7	7	6	6	6	5	5	5	5	4	4	4	4
2.	20	18	17	15	14	13	13	12	11	11	10	9	9	9	8	8	8
3.	30	27	25	23	21	20	19	18	17	16	15	14	14	13	13	12	12
4.	40	36	33	31	29	27	25	24	22	21	20	19	18	17	17	16	15
5.	50	45	42	38	36	33	31	29	28	26	25	24	23	22	21	20	19
6.	60	55	50	46	43	40	38	35	33	32	30	29	27	26	25	24	23
7.	70	64	58	54	50	47	44	41	39	37	35	33	32	30	29	28	27
8.	80	73	67	62	57	53	50	47	44	42	40	38	36	34	33	32	31
9.	90	82	75	69	64	60	56	53	50	47	45	43	41	39	37	36	35
10.	100	91	83	77	71	67	63	59	56	53	50	48	45	43	42	40	39
11.		100	92	85	79	73	69	65	61	58	55	52	50	47	46	44	42
12.			100	92	86	80	75	71	67	63	60	57	54	52	50	48	46
13.				100	93	87	81	76	72	68	65	62	59	56	55	52	50
14.					100	93	88	82	78	74	70	67	63	60	59	56	54
15.						100	94	87	83	79	75	71	68	65	63	60	58
16.							100	94	89	84	80	76	72	69	67	64	62
17.								100	94	89	85	81	77	73	71	68	65
18.									100	95	90	86	81	78	75	72	69
19.										100	95	91	86	82	79	76	73
20.											100	95	90	86	83	80	77
21.												100	95	90	87	84	81
22.													100	95	92	88	85
23.														100	96	92	88
24.															100	96	92
25.																100	96
26.																	100

ACTUAL RIGHT ANSWERS ↓

3. Write the number correct in the space provided.

4. Use the percentage chart to determine the child's accuracy level and write that number in the space provided.

5. Reevaluate the child's performance in terms of patterns of errors. Check those patterns observed.

6. Make any additional comments desired in the space provided.

Record Sheet and Checklist—Pretest

1. After completing and scoring the phonic analysis inventories administered, turn to the "Individual Phonic Analysis Test Record" on page 6 and the "Checklist of Specific Skill Weaknesses" on page 7.

2. Fill in the percentage scores on the record sheet under the PRETEST column. A percentage score of 80% or below indicates an area of weakness.

3. Mark the patterns of errors on the master checklist. Mark the PRETEST with an X.

4. Fill in any recommendations under RECOMMENDATIONS.

5. Use the master record sheet and checklist while preparing the child's remediation.

Record Sheet and Checklist—Posttest

1. Readminister and score the inventories following the same procedure as in pretesting.

2. Fill in the percentage scores under POSTTEST.

3. Compare the child's POSTTEST score and PRETEST score to see if there has been improvement or regression. Subtract the lower score from the higher score.

4. Enter this number under DEVIATION with a plus (+) if improvement is shown (POSTTEST higher than PRETEST) or with a minus (−) if regression occurs (PRETEST higher than POSTTEST). If the PRETEST score and the POSTTEST score are the same, enter a zero (0) under DEVIATION.

Example:

Matching Initial Sounds in Words	PRETEST	POSTTEST	DEVIATION
Child A	47%	87%	+40%
Child B	98%	98%	0
Child C	80%	73%	−7%

5. Mark the patterns of errors found on the checklist. Use a check mark for POSTTEST.

6. Write recommendations in the space provided.

7. Use the checklist for further remediation exercises.

Individual Phonic Analysis Test Record

NAME _____ GRADE __ TEACHER _____

PRETEST DATE _____ POSTTEST DATE _____ SCHOOL _____

Test	Pretest	Posttest	Deviation
A. Letter Discrimination—Upper Case/ Lower Case			
B. Recognizing Initial Letters in Words			
C. Recognizing Final Letters in Words			
D. Recognizing Medial Letters in Words			
E. Recognizing Rhymes in Words; Recognizing Word Family Rhymes			
F. Matching Initial, Final, and Medial Sounds in Words			
G. Matching Two-Letter Blending Sounds and Consonant Digraph Sounds in the Initial and Final Positions			
H. Matching Three-Letter Initial Blends			
I. Matching Vowel Sounds (Includes Digraphs and Diphthongs)			
J. Recognizing Consonant Blends and Digraphs in the Initial and Final Positions			
K. Marking Vowels Long and Short			
L. Recognizing Y as a Consonant and as a Vowel			
M. Applying Vowel Rules (CVC and CVCe)			
N. Applying Vowel Rules (CV and CVVC)			
O. Applying Vowel Rule Exceptions (Parts One and Two)			
P. Matching Words with the Sounds of C, G, and S			
Q. Marking Nonsense Words According to Vowel Rules			

Checklist of Specific Skill Weaknesses
Phonic Analysis

NAME _____ GRADE __ TEACHER _____

PRETEST DATE _____ POSTTEST DATE _____ SCHOOL _____

PATTERNS OF ERRORS   Pretest Weakness = X
Posttest Weakness = ✔

Levels – A, B, C, D, and certain ones in F

_____ Inability to recognize lower case letters
_____ Inability to recognize upper case letters
_____ Reverses letters
_____ Inverts letters
_____ Inability to recognize letters in initial position
_____ Inability to recognize letters in medial position
_____ Inability to recognize letters in final position

Levels – Some B, and some C

_____ Inability to name letters
_____ Inability to give initial consonant sound
_____ Inability to give final consonant sound
_____ Inability to give medial vowel sound

Levels – E – Q

_____ Inability to recognize word families as rhymes
_____ Inability to recognize initial two-letter blends
_____ Inability to recognize initial three-letter blends
_____ Inability to recognize initial consonant digraphs
_____ Inability to recognize final consonant blends
_____ Inability to recognize final consonant digraphs
_____ Inability to recognize rhymes in words
_____ Inability to match similar initial sounds
_____ Inability to match similar final sounds
_____ Inability to match similar medial sounds
_____ Inability to match initial position blends and digraphs
_____ Inability to match final position blends and digraphs
_____ Inability to match three-letter initial position blends
_____ Inability to match short vowel sounds
_____ Inability to match long vowel sounds
_____ Inability to match vowel digraphs and diphthongs

7

_____ Inability to distinguish between long and short sounds of vowels
_____ Inability to recognize CVC vowels with accuracy
_____ Inability to recognize CVCe vowels with accuracy
_____ Inability to recognize CVVC vowels with accuracy
_____ Inability to recognize CV vowels with accuracy
_____ Inability to recognize Y as a vowel
_____ Inability to recognize Y as a consonant
_____ Inability to recognize CVC rule when applied
_____ Inability to recognize CVCe rule when applied
_____ Inability to recognize CV rule when applied
_____ Inability to recognize CVVC rule when applied
_____ Inability to recognize schwa sound
_____ Inability to recognize o followed by ld or lt vowel rule exception
_____ Inability to recognize i followed by nd, gh or ld vowel rule exception
_____ Inability to recognize a followed by l, ll, w, and u vowel rule exception
_____ Inability to recognize the sound of a vowel followed by r
_____ Inability to recognize the sound of y when it is on the end of a one
        syllable word that contains no other vowel
_____ Inability to recognize the sound of y when it is on the end of a two-syllable
        or more-than-two-syllable word
_____ Inability to match the sounds of c
_____ Inability to match the sounds of g
_____ Inability to match the sounds of s

OBSERVATIONS:

RECOMMENDATIONS:

8

Phonic Analysis

NAME _____ GRADE __ TEACHER _____

DATE _____ SCHOOL _____

LEVEL A – LETTER DISCRIMINATION – UPPER CASE
LETTER DISCRIMINATION – LOWER CASE

Match the letters on the right with those on the left. Write the number of the matching letters on the blank provided.

1.___	C	1. Q	14.___	p	1. r		
2.___	G	2. A	15.___	b	2. b		
		3. G			3. p		
3.___	Q	4. C	16.___	r	4. d		
4.___	O	5. O	17.___	d	5. o		
5.___	I	1. U	18.___	a	1. v		
6.___	T	2. L	19.___	v	2. a		
		3. J			3. h		
7.___	L	4. I	20.___	y	4. j		
8.___	U	5. T	21.___	j	5. y		
9.___	N	1. X	22.___	m	1. n		
10.___	F	2. N	23.___	w	2. z		
		3. K			3. m		
11.___	E	4. F	24.___	n	4. y		
12.___	K	5. E	25.___	z	5. w		
		6. M			6. s		
13.___	X		26.___	s			

PATTERNS OF ERRORS

_____ Inability to recognize lower case letters

_____ Inability to recognize upper case letters

_____ Reverses letters

_____ Inverts letters

COMMENTS: _____

LEVEL A

Number possible _____26_____

Number correct _____

Accuracy _____

Phonic Analysis

NAME _____ GRADE __ TEACHER _____

DATE _____ SCHOOL _____

LEVEL B – RECOGNIZING INITIAL LETTERS IN WORDS
Print the beginning letter of each word on the blank provided and say the letter's <u>name</u> aloud to your teacher.

1. ___ boy	3. ___ saw	5. ___ very	7. ___ ice	9. ___ look
2. ___ fish	4. ___ quick	6. ___ zebra	8. ___ nice	10. ___ made

LEVEL C — RECOGNIZING FINAL LETTERS IN WORDS
Print the ending letter of each word on the blank provided and say the letter's <u>name</u> aloud to your teacher.

1. ___ fox	3. ___ picnic	5. ___ flu	7. ___ sleep	9. ___ slow
2. ___ tub	4. ___ ball	6. ___ bath	8. ___ dog	10. ___ fluff

LEVEL D — RECOGNIZING MEDIAL LETTERS IN WORDS
Print the middle letter(s) of each word on the blank provided and say the letter(s)' <u>name(s)</u> aloud to your teacher.

1. ___ kit	3. ___ boat	5. ___ row	7. ___ sat	9. ___ run
2. ___ dog	4. ___ pet	6. ___ gun	8. ___ float	10. ___ treat

PATTERNS OF ERRORS   LEVEL B

_____ Inability to recognize letters in initial position   Number possible __10__
_____ Inability to recognize letters in final position   Number correct   _____
_____ Inability to recognize letters in medial position   Accuracy   _____

LEVEL C

Number possible __10__
Number correct   _____
Accuracy   _____

LEVEL D

Number possible __10__
Number correct   _____
Accuracy   _____

COMMENTS: _____

Phonic Analysis

NAME _____ GRADE __ TEACHER _____

DATE _____ SCHOOL _____

LEVEL E – RECOGNIZING RHYMES IN WORDS

Look at the word on the left. Find the words on the right that rhyme with it and write the numbers of the words on the blank provided.

1. ___ BAT	(1) cat	(2) hat	(3) hot
2. ___ CAN	(1) man	(2) fin	(3) fan
3. ___ BALL	(1) wall	(2) tell	(3) tall
4. ___ IT	(1) hit	(2) fit	(3) met

LEVEL E – RECOGNIZING WORD FAMILY RHYMES

Look at the word on the left. Find the words on the right that rhyme with it and write the numbers of the words on the blank provided.

5. ___ LOOK	(1) took	(2) seek	(3) crook
6. ___ HOT	(1) net	(2) not	(3) spot
7. ___ IN	(1) fin	(2) win	(3) men
8. ___ SUN	(1) run	(2) fun	(3) sum

PATTERNS OF ERRORS   LEVEL E

____ Inability to recognize rhymes in words   Number possible __16__
____ Inability to recognize word families as rhymes Number correct _____
____ Deficiency in both areas   Accuracy   _____

COMMENTS: _____

_____

Phonic Analysis

NAME _____ GRADE __ TEACHER _____

DATE _____ SCHOOL _____

** LEVEL F – MATCHING INITIAL SOUNDS IN WORDS
Look at each word (1,2,3,4) printed below. Listen as your teacher reads orally a group of three words, two of which match the beginning sound of the printed word. On the blank provided, print the numbers of the two words that have the same beginning sound as the printed word.

Example _____ CAT
1. _____ MUD
2. _____ WIND
3. _____ GOAT
4. _____ TIME

** LEVEL F – MATCHING FINAL SOUNDS IN WORDS
Look at each word (5,6,7,8) printed below. Listen as your teacher reads orally a group of three words, two of which match the final sound of the printed word. On the blank provided, print the numbers of the two words that have the same final sound as the printed word.

Example _____ FLAT
5. _____ RAM
6. _____ PILL
7. _____ LUCK
8. _____ GUESS

** LEVEL F – MATCHING MEDIAL SOUNDS IN WORDS
Look at each word (9,10,11,12) printed below. Listen as your teacher reads orally a group of three words, two of which match the medial sound of the printed word. On the blank provided, print the numbers of the two words that have the same medial sound as the printed word.

Example _____ LETTER
9. _____ RIDDLE
10. _____ MANNERS
11. _____ FOLLOW
12. _____ TICKLE

PATTERNS OF ERRORS	LEVEL F	
____ Inability to match similar initial sounds	Number possible	24
____ Inability to recognize initial position	Number correct	_____
____ Inability to match similar final sounds	Accuracy	_____
____ Inability to recognize final position		
____ Inability to match similar medial sounds		
____ Inability to recognize medial position		
____ Deficiency in all areas		

COMMENTS: _____

_____

Phonic Analysis

NAME _____ GRADE __ TEACHER _____

DATE _____ SCHOOL _____

** LEVEL G – MATCHING TWO-LETTER BLENDING SOUNDS AND CON-
SONANT DIGRAPH SOUNDS (INITIAL POSITION)

Look at each word (1,2,3,4,5) printed below. Listen as your teacher reads
orally a group of three words, two of which match the initial two-letter blending sound or consonant digraph sound of the printed word. On the blank
provided, print the numbers of the two words that have the same initial two-
letter blending sound or consonant digraph sound as the printed word.

Example _____ SWAM
1. _____ SHIP
2. _____ STAY
3. _____ PLACE
4. _____ TRAIN
5. _____ WHITE

** LEVEL G – MATCHING TWO-LETTER BLENDING SOUNDS AND CON-
SONANT DIGRAPH SOUNDS (FINAL POSITION)

Look at each word (6,7,8,9,10) printed below. Listen as your teacher reads
orally a group of three words, two of which match the final two-letter blending
sound or consonant digraph sound of the printed word. On the blank provided,
print the numbers of the two words that have the same final two-letter blending sound or consonant digraph sound as the printed word.

Example _____ BLACK
6. _____ THINK
7. _____ DUCK
8. _____ SING
9. _____ SAND
10. _____ MIST

PATTERNS OF ERRORS   LEVEL G

____ Inability to match initial position blends   Number possible   __20__
and digraphs   Number correct   _____
____ Inability to match final position blends   Accuracy   _____
and digraphs
____ Deficiency in both areas

COMMENTS: _____

_____

Phonic Analysis

NAME _____ GRADE __ TEACHER _____

DATE _____ SCHOOL _____

** LEVEL H – MATCHING THREE-LETTER INITIAL BLENDS

Look at each word (1,2,3,4,5,6,7) printed below. Listen as your teacher reads orally a group of three words, two of which match the beginning three-letter blending sound of the printed word. On the blank provided, print the numbers of the two words that have the same beginning three-letter blending sound as the printed word.

Example _____ STROKE

1 _____ SCRAPE

2. _____ SHRIMP

3. _____ SPLASH

4. _____ SPRAIN

5. _____ SQUEEZE

6. _____ STRANGE

7. _____ THREE

PATTERNS OF ERRORS

_____ Inability to match three-letter initial position blends.

LEVEL H

Number possible   __14__

Number correct   _____

Accuracy   _____

COMMENTS: _____

Phonic Analysis

NAME _____ GRADE __ TEACHER _____

DATE _____ SCHOOL _____

LEVEL I – MATCHING VOWEL SOUNDS (INCLUDES DIGRAPHS AND DIPHTHONGS)

Look at the word on the left. Find the words on the right that have the same vowel sound. Write the numbers of the words on the blank provided.

_____

1. ___ RIDE   (1) time   (2) hit   (3) ripe

2. ___ CUB   (1) tune   (2) but   (3) sun

3. ___ HAT   (1) jam   (2) game   (3) map

4. ___ DOT   (1) hop   (2) rope   (3) stop

5. ___ MEAT   (1) set   (2) dream   (3) speak

6. ___ BOAT   (1) croak   (2) cot   (3) coat

7. ___ MOUSE   (1) house   (2) out   (3) float

_____
_____

PATTERNS OF ERRORS	LEVEL I

____ Inability to match short vowel sounds   Number possible __14__

____ Inability to match long vowel sounds´   Number correct ____

____ Inability to match vowel digraph and diphthong   Accuracy ____
     sounds

____ Deficiency in all areas

COMMENTS: _____

_____

Phonic Analysis

NAME _____ GRADE __ TEACHER _____

DATE _____ SCHOOL _____

LEVEL J – RECOGNIZING CONSONANT BLENDS AND DIGRAPHS (INITIAL POSITION)

Listen to each word as it is read aloud and identify the letters that make the blending sound at the beginning of each word.

Example: Your teacher reads the word <u>share</u>. You identify the letters <u>s</u> and <u>h</u> as making the <u>sh</u> sound.

1. ___ sheep
2. ___ plan
3. ___ wheat
4. ___ flip
5. ___ stream

6. ___ string
7. ___ trout
8. ___ thing
9. ___ sprain
10. ___ scratch

LEVEL J – RECOGNIZING CONSONANT BLENDS AND DIGRAPHS (FINAL POSITION)

Listen to each word as it is read aloud and identify the letters that make the blending sound at the end of each word.

Example: Your teacher reads the word <u>tack</u>. You identify the letters <u>c</u> and <u>k</u> as making the <u>ck</u> sound.

11. ___ lamp
12. ___ smash
13. ___ bank
14. ___ task
15. ___ lunch

16. ___ pack
17. ___ wish
18. ___ song
19. ___ wasp
20. ___ punch

PATTERNS OF ERRORS

_____ Inability to recognize initial two-letter blends

_____ Inability to recognize initial three-letter blends

_____ Inability to recognize initial consonant digraphs

_____ Inability to recognize final consonant blends

_____ Inability to recognize final consonant digraphs

_____ Deficiency in all areas

LEVEL J

Number possible __20__
Number correct ____
Accuracy ____

COMMENTS: _____

_____

Phonic Analysis

NAME _____ GRADE __ TEACHER _____

DATE _____ SCHOOL _____

LEVEL K – MARKING VOWELS LONG AND SHORT

Look at each word and say it to yourself. Decide if the underlined vowel has a long or short sound. In the blank provided, write (L) for long vowel or (S) for short vowel.

_____

1. ___ c<u>a</u>t

2. ___ sl<u>i</u>de

3. ___ c<u>u</u>te

4. ___ r<u>u</u>g

5. ___ b<u>e</u>d

6. ___ t<u>a</u>ke

7. ___ g<u>oa</u>t

8. ___ r<u>oa</u>m

9. ___ m<u>e</u>

10. ___ c<u>a</u>me

11. ___ f<u>i</u>t

12. ___ sh<u>e</u>

13. ___ w<u>e</u>t

14. ___ r<u>o</u>pe

15. ___ d<u>i</u>me

_____

PATTERNS OF ERRORS	LEVEL K

PATTERNS OF ERRORS

____ Inability to distinguish between long and short sounds of vowels
____ Inability to recognize CVC vowels with accuracy
____ Inability to recognize CVCe vowels with accuracy
____ Inability to recognize CVVC vowels with accuracy
____ Inability to recognize CV vowels with accuracy
____ Deficiency in all areas

LEVEL K

Number possible __15__
Number correct ____
Accuracy ____

Teacher's Note: If the child cannot pronounce the words, read the words aloud and then ask the student to mark the vowels.

COMMENTS: _____

_____

Phonic Analysis

NAME _____ GRADE __ TEACHER _____

DATE _____ SCHOOL _____

LEVEL L – RECOGNIZING Y AS A CONSONANT AND AS A VOWEL

Listen as your teacher reads aloud each of the words below. In each of the words, Y is acting like a consonant or like a vowel. If Y is acting like a vowel, place a V on the blank beside the word. If Y is acting like a consonant, place a C in the blank beside the word.

Example: pretty ____V____

---

1. ___ yard   6. ___ apply   11. ___ yarn

2. ___ gym   7. ___ my   12. ___ candy

3. ___ yeast   8. ___ yet   13. ___ hilly

4. ___ cycle   9. ___ penny   14. ___ yacht

5. ___ yawn   10. ___ crystal   15. ___ silly

PATTERNS OF ERRORS   LEVEL L

____ Inability to recognize Y as a vowel   Number possible __15__
____ Inability to recognize Y as a consonant   Number correct _____
____ Deficiency in both areas   Accuracy   _____

COMMENTS: _____

_____

© 1985 by Parker Publishing Company, Inc.

Phonic Analysis

NAME _____ GRADE __ TEACHER _____

DATE _____ SCHOOL _____

LEVEL M – APPLYING VOWEL RULES

The vowels in these words are marked for you. Below are rules for marking vowels. Look at each word and decide which rule best tells why each word is marked as it is. Write the letter of the correct rule on the blank beside each word.

---

1. jĕt ____

2. tĕn ____

3. bōne̸ ____

4. mūle̸ ____

5. tōne̸ ____

6. gāte̸ ____

7. nīne̸ ____

8. tĭp ____

9. nāme̸ ____

10. măp ____

11. băt ____

12. cūbe̸ ____

13. hŏt ____

14. wĕt ____

15. cāpe̸ ____

RULES

A. If a one-syllable word has a single-vowel letter between two consonant letters, that vowel letter usually represents its short sound. (CVC = Short Vowel Sound). Example: cat

B. If a one-syllable word has a single-vowel letter between two consonant letters and it ends in –e, the vowel letter usually represents its long sound and the –e is silent. (CVCe = Long Vowel Sound and Silent e). Example: fame

---

PATTERNS OF ERRORS

____ Inability to recognize CVC rule when applied
____ Inability to recognize CVCe rule when applied
____ Deficiency in both areas

LEVEL M

Number possible __15__
Number correct ____
Accuracy ____

COMMENTS: _____

_____

Phonic Analysis

NAME _____ GRADE __ TEACHER _____

DATE _____ SCHOOL _____

LEVEL N – APPLYING VOWEL RULES

The vowels in these words are marked for you. Below are rules for marking vowels. Look at each word and decide which rule best tells why each word is marked as it is. Write the letter of the correct rule in the blank beside each word.

---

1. dēep ___   6. wē ___   11. sō ___

2. bēad ___   7. pāin ___   12. sōak ___

3. mē ___   8. shē ___   13. rāid ___

4. sēe ___   9. nō ___   14. fōam ___

5. bē ___   10. sēem ___   15. lēad ___

RULES

A. When a one-syllable word ends in a vowel letter, that vowel letter usually represents its long sound (CV = Long Vowel Sound). Example: me

B. When two vowel letters come together, the first letter is usually long and the second letter is usually silent. (CVVC = Long Vowel Sound for first vowel and Silent Vowel for the second vowel letter). Example: boat

---

PATTERNS OF ERRORS

___ Inability to recognize CV rule when applied
___ Inability to recognize CVVC rule when applied
___ Deficiency in both areas

LEVEL N

Number possible __15__
Number correct ____
Accuracy ____

COMMENTS: _____

Phonic Analysis

NAME _____ GRADE __ TEACHER _____

DATE _____ SCHOOL _____

LEVEL O – APPLYING VOWEL RULE EXCEPTIONS (PART I)

The vowels in these words are marked for you. Below are the rules for marking the vowels. Look at each word and decide which rule best tells why each word is marked as it is. Write the letter of the correct rule in the blank beside each word.

_____

1. bōld ___   6. drâwn ___

2. cōlt ___   7. Pâul ___

3. fīnd ___   8. jōlt ___

4. mīld ___   9. câll

5. tâlk ___   10. chīld ___

VOWEL RULE EXCEPTIONS

A. If the vowel letter o is followed by ld or lt, it usually represents the long sound.

B. If the vowel letter i is followed by nd, gh, ld, it frequently represents the long sound.

C. The letter a has the sound o (aw) when it is followed by l, ll, w, u.

_____

_____

PATTERNS OF ERRORS (PART I)

_____ Inability to recognize o followed by ld or lt vowel rule exception.

_____ Inability to recognize i followed by nd, gh, ld vowel rule exception.

_____ Inability to recognize a followed by l, ll, w, and u vowel rule exception.

_____ Deficiency in all areas.

COMMENTS: _____

_____

Phonic Analysis

NAME _____ GRADE __ TEACHER _____

DATE _____ SCHOOL _____

LEVEL O – APPLYING VOWEL RULE EXCEPTIONS (PART II)

The vowels in these words are marked for you. Below are the rules for marking the vowels. Look at each word and decide which rule best tells why each word is marked as it is. Write the letter of the correct rule in the blank beside each word.

---

1. cär ____
2. mȳ ____
3. windȳ ____
4. nôrth ____
5. flȳ ____

6. rockȳ ____
7. undër ____
8. jellȳ ____
9. drȳ ____
10. badlȳ ____

VOWEL RULE EXCEPTIONS

D. When a vowel or vowels is followed by the letter r, it has a blended sound that is neither the long nor the short sound of the vowel.

E. When a word ends with y and no other vowel is contained in the word, the y functions as a vowel.

F. When y is on the end of a word which has two or more syllables, it has the long e sound.

PATTERNS OF ERRORS (PART II)

____ Inability to recognize the sound of a vowel followed by r.
____ Inability to recognize the sound of y when it is on the end of a one-syllable word that contains no other vowel.
____ Inability to recognize the sound of y when it is on the end of a two or more syllable word.
____ Deficiency in all areas

LEVEL O (PARTS I and II)

Number possible	20
Number correct	_____
Accuracy	_____

COMMENTS: _____

Phonic Analysis

NAME _____ GRADE __ TEACHER _____

DATE _____ SCHOOL _____

LEVEL P – MATCHING WORDS WITH THE SOUND OF C

Look at the words on the left. Find the words on the right that have the same sound of c. Write the numbers of the words in the blanks provided.

1. ___ call	1. cake	2. circle	3. came
2. ___ city	1. cent	2. cycle	3. come
3. ___ cold	1. cup	2. civic	3. cop
4. ___ color	1. cotton	2. cape	3. cyst

LEVEL P – MATCHING WORDS WITH THE SOUND OF G

Look at the words on the left. Find the words on the right that have the same sound of g. Write the numbers of the words in the blank provided.

5. ___ game	1. gum	2. gem	3. goat
6. ___ general	1. got	2. giant	3. germ
7. ___ garnish	1. guard	2. garment	3. gelatin
8. ___ genuine	1. gang	2. gent	3. geometry

LEVEL P – MATCHING WORDS WITH THE SOUND OF S

Look at the word on the left. Find the words on the right that have the same sound of s. Write the numbers of the words in the blank provided.

9. ___ said	1. sing	2. sure	3. soap
10. ___ his	1. has	2. us	3. fives
11. ___ set	1. soap	2. said	3. rose
12. ___ names	1. cheese	2. site	3. is

PATTERNS OF ERRORS   LEVEL P

____ Inability to match the sounds of C.   Number possible __24__
____ Inability to match the sounds of G.   Number correct   ____
____ Inability to match the sounds of S.   Accuracy   ____
____ Deficiency in all areas.

Teacher's Note: If the child cannot pronounce the words, read the words orally and then ask the student to identify the correct sounds. Place the appropriate number of the words in the blank provided.

COMMENTS: _____

Phonic Analysis

NAME _____ GRADE __ TEACHER _____

DATE _____ SCHOOL _____

LEVEL Q – MARKING NONSENSE WORDS ACCORDING TO VOWEL RULES

Look at each nonsense word and say it to yourself. Decide if the underlined vowel letter or vowel combinations represent a long, short, silent or schwa sound. In the blank provided, write (L) for long, (S) for short, (P) for silent, or (Z) for schwa.

_____

1. ___ z<u>ea</u>t   6. ___ f<u>u</u>m   11. ___ p<u>o</u>

2. ___ f<u>o</u>de   7. ___ j<u>a</u>pe   12. ___ w<u>oa</u>p

3. ___ <u>a</u> no'   8. ___ zan'<u>i</u>ty   13. ___ st<u>i</u>ke

4. ___ ch<u>i</u>   9. ___ sh<u>a</u>ne   14. ___ gr<u>u</u>t

5. ___ str<u>oa</u>t   10. ___ <u>i</u>'gent   15. ___ thr<u>u</u>m

_____

_____

PATTERNS OF ERRORS

_____ Inability to mark CVC nonsense words

_____ Inability to mark CVCe nonsense words

_____ Inability to mark CVVC nonsense words

_____ Inability to mark CV nonsense words

_____ Inability to mark the schwa sound in nonsense words

COMMENTS: _____

LEVEL Q

Number possible __15_

Number correct ____

Accuracy ____

ANSWER KEY AND DIRECTIONS
FOR THE PHONIC ANALYSIS INVENTORIES

Level A

1. 4	8. 1	14. 3	21. 4
2. 3	9. 2	15. 2	22. 3
3. 1	10. 4	16. 1	23. 5
4. 5	11. 5	17. 4	24. 1
5. 4	12. 3	18. 2	25. 2
6. 5	13. 1	19. 1	26. 6
7. 2		20. 5	

Level B

1. b	4. q	7. i	9. l
2. f	5. v	8. n	10. m
3. s	6. z		

Level C

1. x	4. l	7. p	9. w
2. b	5. u	8. g	10. f
3. c	6. h		

Level D

1. i	4. e	7. a	9. u
2. o	5. o	8. oa	10. ea
3. oa	6. u		

Level E

1. 1,2	3. 1,3	5. 1,3	7. 1,2
2. 1,3	4. 1,2	6. 2,3	8. 1,2

LEVEL F – MATCHING INITIAL SOUNDS IN WORDS

Read the following words orally to the pupil. Read the stimulus word first and each of the test words (mud-nut, mud-met, mud-mice). Pause between each set of words long enough for the pupil to mark his or her response in the appropriate blank. Follow this procedure for each of the words presented in the exercise. Before beginning the exercise, do the example item with the pupil and answer any questions that may be asked.

Example:

cat	(1) cent	(2) cup	(3) can

---

1. mud	(1) nut	(2) met	(3) mice
2. wind	(1) wagon	(2) which	(3) wash
3. goat	(1) girl	(2) get	(3) germ
4. time	(1) though	(2) too	(3) talk

LEVEL F – MATCHING FINAL SOUNDS IN WORDS

Read the following words orally to the pupil. Read the stimulus word first and each of the test words (ram-rim, ram-tin, ram-sam). Pause between each set of words long enough for the pupil to mark his or her response in the appropriate blank. Follow this procedure for each of the words presented in the exercise. Before beginning the exercise, do the example item with the pupil and answer any questions that may be asked.

Example:

flat	(1) mat	(2) fan	(3) hat

5. ram	(1) rim	(2) tin	(3) sam
6. pill	(1) tar	(2) shell	(3) tall
7. luck	(1) knock	(2) not	(3) book
8. guess	(1) buzz	(2) miss	(3) fuss

LEVEL F – MATCHING MEDIAL SOUNDS IN WORDS

Read the following words orally to the pupil. Read the stimulus word first and each of the test words (riddle-fiddle, riddle-bubble, riddle-middle). Pause between each set of words long enough for the pupil to mark his or her response in the appropriate blank. Follow this procedure for each of the words presented in the exercise. Before beginning the exercise, do the example item with the pupil and answer any questions that may be asked.

Example:

letter	(1) better	(2) kitten	(3) yellow

9. riddle	(1) fiddle	(2) bubble	(3) middle
10. manners	(1) dinner	(2) canning	(3) simmer
11. follow	(1) hollow	(2) collar	(3) bottom
12. tickle	(1) million	(2) picket	(3) kicker

LEVEL G – MATCHING TWO-LETTER BLENDING SOUNDS AND CONSONANT DIGRAPH SOUNDS (INITIAL POSITION)

Read the following words orally to the pupil. Read the stimulus word first and each of the test words (ship-she, ship-wish, ship-shadow). Pause between each set of words long enough for the pupil to mark his or her response in the appropriate blank. Follow this procedure for each of the words presented in the exercise. Before beginning the exercise, do the example item with the pupil and answer any questions that may be asked.

Example:

swam	(1) swap	(2) sat	(3) swim

1. ship	(1) she	(2) wish	(3) shadow
2. stay	(1) start	(2) stick	(3) skate
3. place	(1) please	(2) promise	(3) plank
4. train	(1) trap	(2) trip	(3) twin
5. white	(1) wheat	(2) where	(3) shower

LEVEL G – MATCHING TWO-LETTER BLENDING SOUNDS AND CONSONANT DIGRAPH SOUNDS (FINAL POSITION)

Read the following words orally to the pupil. Read the stimulus word first and each of the test words (think-drank, think-bunk, think-thing). Pause between each set of words long enough for the pupil to mark his or her response in the appropriate blank. Follow this procedure for each of the words presented in the exercise. Before beginning the exercise, do the example item with the pupil and answer any questions that may be asked.

Example:

black	(1) back	(2) brick	(3) sand

6. think	(1) drank	(2) bunk	(3) thing
7. duck	(1) pick	(2) stock	(3) clump
8. sing	(1) rang	(2) blank	(3) strong
9. sand	(1) strong	(2) wind	(3) bond
10. mist	(1) digest	(2) insist	(3) crisp

LEVEL H – MATCHING THREE-LETTER INITIAL BLENDS

Read the following words orally to the pupil. Read the stimulus word first and each of the test words (scrape-scratch, scrape-squirt, scrape-screen). Pause between each set of words long enough for the pupil to mark his or her response in the appropriate blank. Follow this procedure for each of the words presented in the exercise. Before beginning the exercise, do the example item with the pupil, and answer any questions that may be asked.

Example:

stroke	(1) strung	(2) stop	(3) struck

1. scrape	(1) scratch	(2) squirt	(3) screen
2. shrimp	(1) scrap	(2) shred	(3) shrug
3. splash	(1) split	(2) splice	(3) sprang
4. sprain	(1) spring	(2) sprinkle	(3) splinter
5. squeeze	(1) square	(2) scrawny	(3) squeak
6. strange	(1) spray	(2) strong	(3) street
7. three	(1) throat	(2) thread	(3) that

Level I

1. 1,3
2. 2,3
3. 1,3
4. 1,3
5. 2,3
6. 1,3
7. 1,2

Level J

1. sh	6. str
2. pl	7. tr
3. wh	8. th
4. fl	9. spr
5. str	10. scr

11. mp	16. ck
12. sh	17. sh
13. nk	18. ng
14. sk	19. sp
15. ch	20. ch

Level K

1. S	4. S	7. L	10. L	13. S
2. L	5. S	8. L	11. S	14. L
3. L	6. L	9. L	12. L	15. L

Level L

1. C	4. V	7. V	10. V	13. V
2. V	5. C	8. C	11. C	14. C
3. C	6. V	9. V	12. V	15. V

Level M

1. A	4. B	7. B	10. A	13. A
2. A	5. B	8. A	11. A	14. A
3. B	6. B	9. B	12. B	15. B

LEVEL N

1. B	4. B	7. B	10. B	13. B
2. B	5. A	8. A	11. A	14. B
3. A	6. A	9. A	12. B	15. B

LEVEL O (PART I)

1. A	3. B	5. C	7. C	9. C
2. A	4. B	6. C	8. A	10. B

LEVEL O (PART II)

1. D	3. F	5. E	7. D	9. E
2. E	4. D	6. F	8. F	10. F

LEVEL P

1. 1,3	4. 1,2	7. 1,2	10. 1,3
2. 1,2	5. 1,3	8. 2,3	11. 1,2
3. 1,3	6. 2,3	9. 1,3	12. 1,3

LEVEL Q

1. L	4. L	7. L	10. Z	13. L
2. L	5. L	8. Z	11. L	14. S
3. Z	6. S	9. L	12. L	15. S

INFORMAL STRUCTURAL ANALYSIS INVENTORIES

TEACHER'S GUIDE

Introduction

The following informal reading inventories have been designed for the diagnosis of specific tasks in the area of structural analysis. The sequential pattern of skills begins with the matching of letters and concludes with the syllabication of words and the application of syllabication rules. The first two tests, Matching Upper Case Letters and Distinguishing Between Similar Word Forms, and the skills which they assess are not structural analysis skills. However, they have been included to enable the tester who is working with young readers to assess the reader's knowledge of these very basic letters and word discrimination skills. Readers who do not know these skills will probably be unable to complete the tests.

No child is expected to complete the entire series. Some skills may be too advanced, others too easy. The number of skills tested are determined by the examiner. Administering the complete test takes approximately forty minutes.

When completing each sub-test of the Informal Reading Inventories, a child's score is never compared with the score of another child in the room or in another area of the country. The only comparison made is between the child's PRETEST score and his/her POSTTEST score.

Directions

The following are general directions for administering the informal structural analysis inventories.
1. Decide which skills need to be measured and test only those skills.
2. Explain to the child EXACTLY what he/she is expected to do.
3. Administer each skill test separately.
4. Write any immediate comments before administering the next test.
5. Give the child a rest period when needed. Don't expect the student to complete too many tasks at one sitting.

Scoring

1. Refer to the Answer Key on pages 51-52 for the correct answers.
2. Each test has 15 items and follows this percentage chart:

15 items correct — 100%
14 items correct — 93%

13 items correct — 87%
12 items correct — 80%
11 items correct — 73%
10 items correct — 67%
 9 items correct — 60%
 8 items correct — 53%
 7 items correct — 47%
 6 items correct — 40%
 5 items correct — 33%
 4 items correct — 27%
 3 items correct — 20%
 2 items correct — 13%
 1 items correct — 7%

3. Write the number correct in the space provided.

4. Use the percentage chart given above to determine the child's accuracy level and write that number in the space provided.

5. Reevaluate the child's performance in terms of patterns of errors. Check those patterns observed.

6. Make any additional comments desired in the space provided.

Record Sheet and Checklist—Pretest

1. After completing and scoring the structural analysis inventories administered, turn to the "Individual Structural Analysis Test Record" on page 33 and the "Checklist of Specific Skill Weaknesses" on page 34-35.

2. Fill in the percentage scores on the record sheet under the PRETEST column. A percentage score of 80% or below indicates an area of weakness.

3. Mark the patterns of errors on the master checklist. Mark the PRETEST with an X.

4. Fill in any recommendations under RECOMMENDATIONS.

5. Use this master record sheet and checklist while preparing the child's remediation.

Record Sheet and Checklist—Posttest

1. Readminister and score the inventories following the same procedure as in pretesting.

2. Fill in the percentage scores under POSTTEST.

3. Compare the child's POSTTEST score with his or her PRETEST score to see if there has been improvement or regression. Subtract the lower score from the higher score.

4. Enter this number under DEVIATION with a plus (+) if improvement is shown (POSTTEST higher than PRETEST) or with a minus (−) if regression occurs (PRETEST higher than POSTTEST). If the PRETEST score and the POSTTEST score are the same, enter a zero (0) under DEVIATION.

Example:

Dividing Compound Words	PRETEST	POSTTEST	DEVIATION
Child A	47%	80%	+40%
Child B	93%	93%	0
Child C	80%	73%	−7%

5. Mark the patterns of errors found on the checklist. Use a check mark for the POSTTEST.

6. Write recommendations in the space provided.

7. Utilize the checklist for further remediation exercises.

Individual Structural Analysis Test Record

NAME _____ GRADE __ TEACHER _____

PRETEST DATE _____ POSTTEST DATE _____ SCHOOL _____

Test	Pretest	Posttest	Deviation
A. Matching Upper Case Letters			
B. Distinguishing Between Similar Word Forms			
C. Dividing Compound Words			
D. Recognition of Inflectional Word Endings			
E. Contractions – Part One			
F. Contractions – Part Two			
G. Recognizing Root Words			
H. Making Words Plural			
I. Using Possessives and Possessive Pronouns			
J. Recognizing Syllables in Words – Part One			
K. Recognizing Syllables in Words – Part Two			
L. Dividing Words into Syllables – Part One			
M. Applying Syllabication Rules – Part One			
N. Dividing Words into Syllables – Part Two			
O. Applying Syllabication Rules – Part Two			
P. Dividing Words into Syllables – Part Three			
Q. Applying Syllabication Rules – Part Three			

Checklist of Specific Skill Weaknesses
Structural Analysis

NAME _____ GRADE __ TEACHER _____

PRETEST DATE _____ POSTTEST DATE _____ SCHOOL _____

PATTERNS OF ERRORS   Pretest Weakness = X
                            Posttest Weakness = ✔

Levels A – B

____ Inability to distinguish between upper case letters
____ Reverses letters – upper case
____ Inverts letters – upper case
____ Letter reversals within the word
____ Reverses words
____ Ignores initial letter combinations
____ Ignores medial letter combinations
____ Ignores final letter combinations

OBSERVATIONS: _____

_____

Levels C – I
____ Inability to recognize small words in compound words
____ Inability to recognize -s endings
____ Inability to recognize -ed endings
____ Inability to recognize -ing endings
____ Inability to recognize root word from suffix
____ Inability to recognize root word from prefix
____ Inability to distinguish root word from both affixes
____ Inability to match contractions with related word forms
____ Inability to use correct contraction forms in context
____ Inability to form contractions
____ Inability to write words which form contractions
____ Inability to use possessives in context
____ Inability to recognize possessive pronouns
____ Inability to form -s plurals
____ Inability to form -es plurals
____ Inability to form -ies plurals
____ Inability to form -ves plurals

34

OBSERVATIONS: _____

_____

Levels J – Q

____ Inability to recognize one-syllable words
____ Inability to recognize two-syllable words
____ Inability to recognize three-syllable words
____ Inability to recognize four-syllable words
____ Inability to recognize five- and six-syllable words
____ Inability to divide VCV words
____ Inability to divide VCCV words
____ Inability to divide -le words
____ Inability to divide words with consonant blends/digraphs
____ Inability to divide words with single vowel as a syllable
____ Inability to divide words with affixes
____ Inability to divide words with accent on first syllable
____ Inability to recognize VCV rule when applied
____ Inability to recognize VCCV rule when applied
____ Inability to recognize -le rule when applied
____ Inability to recognize a single consonant between vowels rule when applied
____ Inability to recognize affix rule when applied
____ Inability to recognize consonant blend/digraph rule when applied

OBSERVATIONS: _____

_____

RECOMMENDATIONS:

Structural Analysis

NAME _____ GRADE __ TEACHER _____

DATE _____ SCHOOL _____

LEVEL A – MATCHING UPPER CASE LETTERS

Write the number of the letter on the right that is the same as the letter on the left. Write the number in the blank provided.

a.		c.		e.	
K ____	(1) Y	B ____	(7) P	C ____	(13) C
Y ____	(2) K	P ____	(8) R	O ____	(14) D
X ____	(3) X	R ____	(9) B	D ____	(15) O

b.		d.	
W ____	(4) L	A ____	(10) V
L ____	(5) M	N ____	(11) A
M ____	(6) W	V ____	(12) N

© 1985 by Parker Publishing Company, Inc.

PATTERNS OF ERRORS

____ Inability to distinguish between
    upper case letters
____ Reverses letters – upper case
____ Inverts letters – upper case
____ Deficiency in all areas

LEVEL A

Number Possible __15__
Number Correct ____
Accuracy ____

COMMENTS: _____

_____

Structural Analysis

NAME _____ GRADE ____ TEACHER _____

DATE _____ SCHOOL _____

LEVEL B – DISTINGUISHING BETWEEN SIMILAR WORD FORMS

Write the number of the word on the right that is the same as the word on the left. Write the number in the blank provided.

1. ___	no	(1) not	(2) no	(3) on	
2. ___	then	(1) them	(2) then	(3) there	
3. ___	days	(1) sad	(2) day	(3) days	
4. ___	bath	(1) bath	(2) path	(3) that	
5. ___	bead	(1) pump	(2) dead	(3) bead	
6. ___	middle	(1) nibble	(2) middle	(3) meddle	
7. ___	hole	(1) hello	(2) hollow	(3) hole	
8. ___	children	(1) chicken	(2) child	(3) children	
9. ___	imagine	(1) image	(2) machine	(3) imagine	
10. ___	elevator	(1) escalator	(2) elevator	(3) evaluator	
11. ___	bark	(1) dark	(2) crack	(3) bark	(4) back
12. ___	cover	(1) curve	(2) cover	(3) corner	(4) converse
13. ___	biennial	(1) diesel	(2) biennium	(3) bicentennial	(4) biennial
14. ___	analytic	(1) analytical	(2) analysis	(3) analyst	(4) analytic
15. ___	palatal	(1) palate	(2) palatal	(3) palatial	(4) palatable

PATTERNS OF ERRORS

____ Letter reversals within the word
____ Word reversals
____ Ignores initial letter combinations
____ Ignores medial letter combinations
____ Ignores final letter combinations
____ Deficiency in all areas

LEVEL B

Number possible __15__
Number correct ____
Accuracy ____

COMMENTS: _____

Structural Analysis

NAME _____ GRADE __ TEACHER _____

DATE _____ SCHOOL _____

LEVEL C – DIVIDING COMPOUND WORDS

Draw a vertical line between the two words that make one word.

1. bedroom	5. firehouse	9. playhouse	13. bookstore
2. snowball	6. doghouse	10. barnyard	14. something
3. without	7. birthday	11. cowboy	15. firearm
4. henhouse	8. raincoat	12. cookbook	

LEVEL D – RECOGNITION OF INFLECTIONAL WORD ENDINGS

Circle the inflectional ending of each word.

1. looking	5. laughing	9. reads	13. runs
2. played	6. finding	10. painted	14. rides
3. works	7. jumps	11. walked	15. wanted
4. helped	8. seeing	12. called	

PATTERNS OF ERRORS

_____ Inability to recognize small words
     in compound words
_____ Inability to recognize -s endings
_____ Inability to recognize -ed endings
_____ Inability to recognize -ing endings
_____ Deficiency in all areas

LEVEL C

Number possible   _15_
Number correct   _____
Accuracy   _____

LEVEL D

Number possible   _15_
Number correct   _____
Accuracy   _____

COMMENTS: _____

_____

Structural Analysis

NAME _____ GRADE __ TEACHER _____

DATE _____ SCHOOL _____

LEVEL E – CONTRACTIONS

Write in the blank the letter of the two words that are used to form the contraction.

1. I'm ___	(a) it is	5. he's ___	(e) is not
2. it's ___	(b) I am	6. isn't ___	(f) let us
3. we've ___	(c) I have	7. let's ___	(g) he is
4. I've ___	(d) we have	8. you're ___	(h) you are

LEVEL E – CONTRACTIONS

Read the sentence. Write in the blank the letter of the correct contraction for the underlined words in the sentence.

9. She is going to school	(a) She'd	(b) She's	(9) ___
10. I can not find my cat.	(a) can't	(b) couldn't	(10) ___
11. He did not get the ball.	(a) doesn't	(b) didn't	(11) ___
12. He and I are not going to the show.	(a) aren't	(b) isn't	(12) ___
13. Jack was not in the car.	(a) weren't	(b) wasn't	(13) ___
14. I will play in the park today.	(a) I'll	(b) I'm	(14) ___
15. He has not ridden a horse.	(a) hasn't	(b) hadn't	(15) ___

PATTERNS OF ERRORS

___ Inability to match contractions
  with related word forms
___ Inability to use correct contraction
  forms in context.
___ Deficiency in all areas.

COMMENTS: _____

LEVEL E

Number possible __15__
Number correct ___
Accuracy ___

Structural Analysis

NAME _____ GRADE __ TEACHER _____

DATE _____ SCHOOL _____

LEVEL F – CONTRACTIONS

Section A – Write in the blank the letter of the two words that are used to form the contraction.

1. he's _____	(a) has not
2. hadn't _____	(b) he will
3. they'll _____	(c) they have
4. haven't _____	(d) he is
5. they've _____	(e) have not
6. he'll _____	(f) they will
7. hasn't _____	(g) had not

LEVEL F – CONTRACTIONS

Section B – Write the correct contraction for the two words given.

8. can not _____

9. it is _____

10. I will _____

11. you have _____

LEVEL F – CONTRACTIONS

Section C – Write the two words that form the contraction.

12. she's _____

13. couldn't _____

14. they'll _____

15. I'm _____

PATTERNS OF ERRORS

____ Inability to match contractions with related word forms
____ Inability to form contractions
____ Inability to write words which form contractions.
____ Deficiency in all areas.

LEVEL F

Number possible __15__
Number correct ____
Accuracy ____

COMMENTS: _____

© 1985 by Parker Publishing Company, Inc.

Structural Analysis

NAME _____ GRADE __ TEACHER _____

DATE _____ SCHOOL _____

LEVEL G – RECOGNIZING ROOT WORDS

Write the root word for each word in the blank provided.

_____

1. guesses _____   6. wooden _____   11. interstate _____
2. smaller _____   7. dislike _____   12. imperfect _____
3. unhappy _____   8. precook _____   13. movement _____
4. liked _____   9. sweetness _____   14. unkindly _____
5. slowly _____   10. turkeys _____   15. disagreeable _____

LEVEL H – MAKING WORDS PLURAL

Write each word in its plural (meaning more than one) form.

_____

1. car _____   6. city _____   11. guess _____
2. knife _____   7. six _____   12. fly _____
3. box _____   8. wife _____   13. ax _____
4. dress _____   9. boat _____   14. potato _____
5. lady _____   10. kiss _____   15. half _____

_____

PATTERNS OF ERRORS

____ Inability to recognize root word from
        suffix
____ Inability to recognize root word from
        prefix
____ Inability to distinguish root word from
        both affixes
____ Inability to form -s plurals
____ Inability to form -es plurals
____ Inability to form -ies plurals
____ Inability to form -ves plurals
____ Deficiency in all areas.

LEVEL G

Number possible __15__
Number correct ____
Accuracy ____

LEVEL H

Number possible __15__
Number correct ____
Accuracy ____

COMMENTS: _____

_____

Structural Analysis

LEVEL I – USING POSSESSIVES AND POSSESSIVE PRONOUNS
Write the letter of the correct response in the blank provided.

---

a doll that belongs to Kathy
1. _____

    (a) Kathy's doll
    (b) Kathys doll

---

a car that belongs to Dad
2. _____

    (a) Dads car
    (b) Dad's car

---

a tail that belongs to a tiger
3. _____

    (a) it's tail
    (b) its tail

---

a game that belongs to Jan
4. _____

    (a) her game
    (b) her's game

---

a cookbook that belongs to Mom
5. _____

    (a) Moms cookbook
    (b) Mom's cookbook

---

a baseball that belongs to Sam
6. _____

    (a) he's baseball
    (b) his baseball

---

a candy apple that belongs to you
7. _____

    (a) you're candy apple
    (b) your candy apple

---

a tree house that belongs to Dan and Bill
8. _____

    (a) their tree house
    (b) they're tree house

---

a yellow ball that belongs to Bill
9. _____

    (a) Bills ball
    (b) Bill's ball

---

a car that belongs to Mike
10. _____

    (a) he's car
    (b) Mike's car

a collar that belongs to a dog 11. _____	(a) dog's collar (b) they're collar
a car that belongs to us 12. _____	(a) are car (b) our car
a book that belongs to me 13. _____	(a) mine book (b) my book
a dog that belongs to John 14. _____	(a) John's dog (b) Your dog
a coat that belongs to Paul 15. _____	(a) Pauls' coat (b) Paul's coat

PATTERNS OF ERRORS

_____ Inability to use possessives in context
_____ Inability to recognize possessive pronouns

LEVEL I

Number possible _15_
Number correct _____
Accuracy _____

COMMENTS: _____

Structural Analysis

NAME _____ GRADE __ TEACHER _____

DATE _____ SCHOOL _____

LEVEL J – RECOGNIZING SYLLABLES IN WORDS—PART I

Say each word to yourself. Write 1 or 2 in the blank to show the number of syllables each word contains.

1. birthday ____	6. picture ____	11. hopscotch ____
2. car ____	7. school ____	12. kitten ____
3. mother ____	8. dad ____	13. cake ____
4. dog ____	9. baseball ____	14. wagon ____
5. hello ____	10. train ____	15. doll ____

Teacher's Note: If the pupil cannot read the words, you should read them aloud.

LEVEL K – RECOGNIZING SYLLABLES IN WORDS—PART II

Say each word to yourself. On the blank, write the number of syllables in each word.

1. hamburger ____	6. amusement ____	11. basketball ____
2. Indian ____	7. anticipation ____	12. contemplation ____
3. aggravating ____	8. saxophone ____	13. Mediterranean ____
4. America ____	9. invitation ____	14. investigation ____
5. astronomical ____	10. stereophonic ____	15. European ____

Teacher's Note: If the pupil cannot read the words, you should read them aloud.

PATTERNS OF ERRORS

____ Inability to recognize one-syllable words
____ Inability to recognize two-syllable words
____ Inability to recognize three-syllable words
____ Inability to recognize four-syllable words
____ Inability to recognize five-syllable words
____ Inability to recognize six-syllable words
____ Deficiency in all areas

LEVEL J

Number possible _15_
Number correct ____
Accuracy ____

LEVEL K

Number possible _15_
Number correct ____
Accuracy ____

COMMENTS: _____

Structural Analysis

NAME _____ GRADE __ TEACHER _____

DATE _____ SCHOOL _____

LEVEL L – DIVIDING WORDS INTO SYLLABLES—PART I

Divide these words into syllables. Draw a line between the last letter of the first syllable and the first letter of the second syllable.

_____

1. doctor	6. carpet	11. lettuce
2. music	7. open	12. about
3. pilot	8. summer	13. tiger
4. candy	9. lumber	14. curtain
5. spider	10. sofa	15. over

_____
_____

PATTERNS OF ERRORS   LEVEL L

____ Inability to divide VCV words   Number possible __15__

____ Inability to divide VCCV words   Number correct ____

____ Deficiency in both areas   Accuracy ____

COMMENTS: _____

_____

Structural Analysis

NAME _____ GRADE __ TEACHER _____

DATE _____ SCHOOL _____

LEVEL M – APPLYING SYLLABICATION RULES—PART I

These words have been divided for you. The rules for dividing the words are found below. Look at each word and decide which syllabication rule best explains why each word is divided as it is. Write the letter of that rule beside the word.

1. let-ter ____   6. pa-per ____   11. cot-ton ____
2. so-da ____   7. din-ner ____   12. can-cel ____
3. pen-cil ____   8. fla-vor ____   13. mar-ket ____
4. ac-tion ____   9. gar-den ____   14. ma-jor ____
5. si-lent ____   10. lis-ten ____   15. fi-nal ____

SYLLABICATION RULES

A. When the first vowel letter is followed by a single consonant letter, that consonant is USUALLY the beginning of the second syllable. (Vowel – Consonant – Vowel Pattern = Divide before the consonant.) Example: be-side

B. When the first vowel letter is followed by two consonant letters and then another vowel, the first syllable USUALLY ends with the first consonant and the second syllable USUALLY starts with the second consonant. (Vowel – Consonant – Consonant – Vowel Pattern = Divide between the two consonants.) Example: cop-per

PATTERNS OF ERRORS

____ Inability to recognize the VCV rule
  when applied
____ Inability to recognize the VCCV rule
  when applied
____ Deficiency in both areas

LEVEL M

Number possible _15_
Number correct ____
Accuracy ____

COMMENTS: _____

Structural Analysis

NAME _____ GRADE __ TEACHER _____

DATE _____ SCHOOL _____

LEVEL N – DIVIDING WORDS INTO SYLLABLES—PART II

Divide these words into syllables. Draw a line between the last letter of one syllable and the first letter of the next syllable.

---

1. stable	6. single	11. meddle
2. ankle	7. mantel	12. arose
3. about	8. sample	13. item
4. open	9. idea	14. fable
5. candle	10. castle	15. rumble

PATTERNS OF ERRORS

____ Inability to divide -le words
____ Inability to divide words with single
        vowel as a syllable
____ Deficiency in all areas

COMMENTS: _____

LEVEL N

Number possible __15__
Number correct ____
Accuracy ____

Structural Analysis

NAME _____ GRADE __ TEACHER _____

DATE _____ SCHOOL _____

LEVEL O – APPLYING SYLLABICATION RULES—PART II

These words have been divided into syllables for you. Rules for dividing the words into syllables are found below. Look at each word and decide which rule best tells why each word is divided as it is. Write the letter of that rule beside the word.

---

1. fa-ble ____	6. prim-i-tive ____	11. whis-tle ____
2. ho-tel ____	7. tram-ple ____	12. min-u-et ____
3. sprin-kle ____	8. be-gin ____	13. her-i-tage ____
4. fam-i-ly ____	9. pi-lot ____	14. cra-dle ____
5. reg-i-ment ____	10. sta-tion ____	15. be-hind ____

RULES

A. A single-vowel letter can be a single syllable. Example: sim-i-lar

B. When a word ends in -le and a consonant letter appears just before it, that consonant letter USUALLY begins the last syllable. Example: tur-tle

C. A single-consonant letter between vowel letters USUALLY goes with the second vowel. Example: be-side

---

PATTERNS OF ERRORS

____ Inability to recognize -le rule when applied
____ Inability to recognize single consonant
    between vowels rule when applied
____ Inability to recognize single vowel as a
    syllable rule when applied
____ Deficiency in all areas

COMMENTS: _____

LEVEL O

Number possible _15_
Number correct ____
Accuracy ____

Structural Analysis

NAME _____ GRADE __ TEACHER _____

DATE _____ SCHOOL _____

LEVEL P – DIVIDING WORDS INTO SYLLABLES—PART III

Divide these words into syllables. Draw a line between the last letter of one syllable and the first letter of the next syllable.

---

1. unfit	6. feather	11. archer
2. closet	7. robin	12. magic
3. salad	8. nonworker	13. hungry
4. careless	9. sweetness	14. fashion
5. graceful	10. ostrich	15. lemon

PATTERNS OF ERRORS

_____ Inability to divide words with affixes
_____ Inability to divide words with accent on the first syllable
_____ Inability to divide words with consonant blends or digraphs
_____ Deficiency in all areas

COMMENTS: _____

_____

LEVEL P

Number possible ___15___
Number correct _____
Accuracy _____

Structural Analysis

NAME _____ GRADE __ TEACHER _____

DATE _____ SCHOOL _____

LEVEL Q – APPLYING SYLLABICATION RULES—PART III

These words have been divided for you. Rules for dividing the words are found below. Look at each word and decide which syllabication rule best tells why each word is divided as it is. Write the letter of that rule beside the word.

---

1. se-cret _____   6. ma-chine _____   11. love-ly _____

2. phos-phate _____   7. un-like _____   12. com-part-ment ____

3. mar-shal _____   8. weath-er _____   13. dis-place _____

4. proph-et _____   9. coun-try _____   14. un-like-ly _____

5. ath-lete _____   10. ur-chin _____   15. re-port-er _____

SYLLABICATION RULES

A. Affixes are separate syllables which appear before or after the root word. Example: un-happy.

B. Syllables do not divide between consonant blends and digraphs. Example: crick-et

---

PATTERNS OF ERRORS   LEVEL Q

____ Inability to recognize affix rule when applied   Number possible __15_
____ Inability to recognize the consonant blend and   Number correct ____
     digraph rule when applied   Accuracy   ____
____ Deficiency in all areas

COMMENTS: _____

ANSWER KEY FOR THE STRUCTURAL ANALYSIS INVENTORIES

LEVEL A

a. 2	b. 6	c. 9	d. 11	e. 13
1	4	7	12	15
3	5	8	10	14

LEVEL B

1. 2	4. 1	7. 3	10. 2	13. 4
2. 2	5. 3	8. 3	11. 3	14. 4
3. 3	6. 2	9. 3	12. 2	15. 2

LEVEL C

1. bed/room	4. hen/house	7. birth/day	10. barn/yard	13. book/store
2. snow/ball	5. fire/house	8. rain/coat	11. cow/boy	14. some/thing
3. with/out	6. dog/house	9. play/house	12. cook/book	15. fire/arm

LEVEL D

1. ing	4. ed	7. s	10. ed	13. s
2. ed	5. ing	8. ing	11. ed	14. s
3. s	6. ing	9. s	12. ed	15. ed

LEVEL E

1. b	4. c	7. f	10. a	13. b
2. a	5. g	8. h	11. b	14. a
3. d	6. e	9. b	12. a	15. a

LEVEL F

1. d	4. e	7. a	10. I'll	13. could not
2. g	5. c	8. can't	11. you've	14. they will
3. f	6. b	9. it's	12. she is	15. I am

LEVEL G

1. guess	4. like	7. like	10. turkey	13. move
2. small	5. slow	8. cook	11. state	14. kind
3. happy	6. wood	9. sweet	12. perfect	15. agree

LEVEL H

1. cars	4. dresses	7. sixes	10. kisses	13. axes
2. knives	5. ladies	8. wives	11. guesses	14. potatoes
3. boxes	6. cities	9. boats	12. flies	15. halves

LEVEL I

1. a	4. a	7. b	10. b	13. b
2. b	5. b	8. a	11. a	14. a
3. b	6. b	9. b	12. b	15. b

LEVEL J

1. 2	4. 1	7. 1	10. 1	13. 1
2. 1	5. 2	8. 1	11. 2	14. 2
3. 2	6. 2	9. 2	12. 2	15. 1

LEVEL K

1. 3	4. 4	7. 5	10. 5	13. 6
2. 3	5. 5	8. 3	11. 3	14. 5
3. 4	6. 3	9. 4	12. 4	15. 4

LEVEL L

1. doc/tor	4. can/dy	7. o/pen	10. so/fa	13. ti/ger
2. mu/sic	5. spi/der	8. sum/mer	11. let/tuce	14. cur/tain
3. pi/lot	6. car/pet	9. lum/ber	12. a/bout	15. o/ver

LEVEL M

1. B	4. B	7. B	10. B	13. B
2. A	5. A	8. A	11. B	14. A
3. B	6. A	9. B	12. B	15. A

LEVEL N

1. sta/ble	4. o/pen	7. man/tel	10. cas/tle	13. i/tem
2. an/kle	5. can/dle	8. sam/ple	11. med/dle	14. fa/ble
3. a/bout	6. sin/gle	9. i/de/a	12. a/rose	15. rum/ble

LEVEL O

1. B	4. A	7. B	10. C	13. A
2. C	5. A	8. C	11. B	14. B
3. B	6. A	9. C	12. A	15. C

LEVEL P

1. un/fit	4. care/less	7. rob/in	10. os/trich	13. hun/gry
2. clos/et	5. grace/ful	8. non/work/er	11. arch/er	14. fash/ion
3. sal/ad	6. feath/er	9. sweet/ness	12. mag/ic	15. lem/on

LEVEL Q

1. B	4. B	7. A	10. B	13. A
2. B	5. B	8. B	11. A	14. A
3. B	6. B	9. B	12. A	15. A

INFORMAL COMPREHENSION SKILLS INVENTORIES

TEACHER'S GUIDE

Introduction

The following informal reading inventories have been designed for the diagnosis of specific tasks in the area of comprehension. No child is expected to complete the entire series. Some skills may be too advanced, others too easy. The number of skills tested is determined by the examiner.

When completing each sub-test of the Informal Reading Inventories, a child's score is never compared with the score of another child in the room or in another area of the country. The only comparison made is between the child's PRETEST score and his/her POSTTEST score.

Directions

The following are general directions for administering the informal comprehension skills inventories.

1. Decide which skills need to be measured and test only those skills.
2. Explain to the child EXACTLY what he/she is expected to do.
3. Administer each skill test separately.
4. Write any immediate comments before administering the next test.
5. Give the child a rest period when needed. Don't expect the student to complete too many tasks at one sitting.
6. This inventory should be administered to only those children who are reading on a fourth grade reading level or higher.

Scoring

1. Refer to the Answer Key on pages 93-95 for the correct answers.
2. Use the "Conversion Table for Computing Percentage of Accuracy" in converting the number of items correct on each test to percentages. Write the percentages in the accuracy blank on each test.

CONVERSION TABLE FOR COMPUTING PERCENTAGE OF ACCURACY

POSSIBLE RIGHT ANSWERS ⟶

ACTUAL NUMBER RIGHT ⟶

	10	11	12	13	14	15	16	17	18	19	20	21	22	23	24	25	26
1.	10	9	8	8	7	7	6	6	6	5	5	5	5	4	4	4	4
2.	20	18	17	15	14	13	13	12	11	11	10	9	9	9	8	8	8
3.	30	27	25	23	21	20	19	18	17	16	15	14	14	13	13	12	12
4.	40	36	33	31	29	27	25	24	22	21	20	19	18	17	17	16	15
5.	50	45	42	38	36	33	31	29	28	26	25	24	23	22	21	20	19
6.	60	55	50	46	43	40	38	35	33	32	30	29	27	26	25	24	23
7.	70	64	58	54	50	47	44	41	39	37	35	33	32	30	29	28	27
8.	80	73	67	62	57	53	50	47	44	42	40	38	36	34	33	32	31
9.	90	82	75	69	64	60	56	53	50	47	45	43	41	39	37	36	35
10.	100	91	83	77	71	67	63	59	56	53	50	48	45	43	42	40	39
11.		100	92	85	79	73	69	65	61	58	55	52	50	47	46	44	42
12.			100	92	86	80	75	71	67	63	60	57	54	52	50	48	46
13.				100	93	87	81	76	72	68	65	62	59	56	55	52	50
14.					100	93	88	82	78	74	70	67	63	60	59	56	54
15.						100	94	87	83	79	75	71	68	65	63	60	58
16.							100	94	89	84	80	76	72	69	67	64	62
17.								100	94	89	85	81	77	73	71	68	65
18.									100	95	90	86	81	78	75	72	69
19.										100	95	91	86	82	79	76	73
20.											100	95	90	86	83	80	77
21.												100	95	90	87	84	81
22.													100	95	92	88	85
23.														100	96	92	88
24.															100	96	92
25.																100	96
26.																	100

3. Write the number correct in the space provided.

4. Use the percentage chart to determine the child's accuracy level and write that number in the space provided.

5. Reevaluate the child's performance in terms of patterns of errors. Check those patterns observed.

6. Make any additional comments desired in the space provided.

Record Sheet and Checklist — Pretest

1. After completing and scoring the comprehension inventories administered, turn to the "Individual Comprehension Skills Test Record" on

page 56 and the "Checklist of Specific Skill Weaknesses" on page 57.

2. Fill in the percentage scores on the record sheet under the PRETEST column. A percentage score of 80% or below indicates an area of weakness.

3. Mark the patterns of errors on the master checklist. Mark the PRETEST with an X.

4. Fill in any recommendations under RECOMMENDATIONS.

5. Use this master record sheet and checklist while preparing the child's remediation.

Record Sheet and Checklist — Posttest

1. Readminister and score the inventories following the same procedure as in pretesting.

2. Fill in the percentage scores under POSTTEST.

3. Compare the child's POSTTEST score with his or her PRETEST score to see if there has been improvement or regression. Subtract the lower score from the higher score.

4. Enter this number under DEVIATION with a plus (+) if improvement is shown (POSTTEST higher than PRETEST) or with a minus (−) if regression occurs (PRETEST higher than POSTTEST). If the PRETEST score and the POSTTEST score are the same, enter a zero (0) under DEVIATION.

Example:

Understanding Words in Isolation	PRETEST	POSTTEST	DEVIATION
Child A	46%	86%	+40%
Child B	96%	96%	0
Child C	81%	73%	−8%

5. Mark the patterns of errors found on the checklist. Use a check mark for POSTTEST.

6. Write recommendations in the space provided.

7. Utilize the checklist for further remediation exercises.

Individual Comprehension Skills Test Record

NAME _____ GRADE __ TEACHER _____

PRETEST DATE _____ POSTTEST DATE _____ SCHOOL _____

Test	Pretest	Posttest	Deviation
A. Understanding Words in Isolation			
B. Understanding Multiple Meaning Words in Context			
C. Understanding Technical Words in Context			
D. Recalling Facts Read			
E. Following Directions Read			
F. Sequencing Ideas Read			
G. Selecting Important Details			
H. Identifying Main Ideas Not Explicitly Stated			
I. Drawing Logical Conclusions			
J. Predicting Logical Outcomes			
K. Interpreting Key Concepts About Story Characters			
L. Associating the Text with the Correct Picture			
M. Following Plot Sequence			
N. Classifying Information			
O. Determining Cause and Effect Relationships			
P. Summarizing Material Read			
Q. Identifying and Understanding Figures of Speech			
R. Detecting and Interpreting Propaganda Techniques			

Checklist of Specific Skill Weaknesses
Comprehension Skills

NAME _____ GRADE __ TEACHER _____

PRETEST DATE _____ POSTTEST DATE _____ SCHOOL _____

PATTERNS OF ERRORS
Pretest Weakness = X
Posttest Weakness = ✔

Levels A, B, and C

_____ Inability to understand words in isolation
_____ Inability to understand multiple meaning words in context
_____ Inability to understand technical words in context

Levels D, E, F, and G

_____ Inability to recall facts read
_____ Inability to follow directions read
_____ Inability to sequence ideas read
_____ Inability to select important details

Levels H, I, J, K, L, M, N, O, and P

_____ Inability to identify main ideas not explicitly stated
_____ Inability to draw logical conclusions
_____ Inability to predict logical outcomes
_____ Inability to interpret key concepts about story characters
_____ Inability to associate the text with the correct picture
_____ Inability to follow plot sequence
_____ Inability to classify information
_____ Inability to determine cause and effect relationships
_____ Inability to summarize material read

Levels Q and R

_____ Inability to identify and understand figures of speech
_____ Inability to detect and interpret propaganda techniques

OBSERVATIONS:

RECOMMENDATIONS:

Comprehension Skills

NAME _____ GRADE __ TEACHER _____

DATE _____ SCHOOL _____

LEVEL A – UNDERSTANDING WORDS IN ISOLATION

Directions: Match the vocabulary words listed on the left with the correct definition listed on the right. Place the letter of the correct definition in the
blank beside each word.

VOCABULARY WORDS	DEFINITIONS
____ 1. hole	A. to reason
____ 2. think	B. below
____ 3. more	C. astonish
____ 4. under	D. an opening through a thing
____ 5. surprise	E. an additional amount

____ 6. learn	A. sufficient
____ 7. decide	B. resolve
____ 8. foolish	C. gain knowledge
____ 9. enough	D. ridiculous
____ 10. beautiful	E. pretty

____ 11. none	A. gigantic
____ 12. question	B. not any
____ 13. exercise	C. inquiry
____ 14. enormous	D. to break in upon
____ 15. interrupt	E. develop through regular use

____ 16. burst	A. defeat
____ 17. conquer	B. to decide
____ 18. admire	C. riddle
____ 19. determine	D. break apart
____ 20. mystery	E. to esteem highly

____ 21. ascend	A. old
____ 22. ancient	B. enter
____ 23. theory	C. climb
____ 24. penetrate	D. hard to believe
____ 25. incredible	E. hypothesis

PATTERNS OF ERRORS

____ Inability to understand words in isolation

LEVEL A

Number possible __25__

Number correct ____

Accuracy ____

COMMENTS: _____

_____

Comprehension Skills

NAME _____ GRADE ____ TEACHER _____

DATE _____ SCHOOL _____

LEVEL B – UNDERSTANDING MULTIPLE MEANING WORDS IN CONTEXT

Directions: Read the following sentences carefully. In the blank provided, write the letter of the phrase or word that has the correct meaning for the underlined word. Be sure the meaning chosen is appropriate for the way the word is used in the sentence.

_____ 1. The officer asked the man to <u>state</u> how he was involved in the robbery.

    A. one of the constituent units of a nation
    B. to express in words
    C. condition of being

_____ 2. The man carefully examined his sore finger and found that he had <u>run</u> a wooden splinter into the skin.

    A. to cause to penetrate
    B. to carry on
    C. to go at full speed

_____ 3. The waiter <u>grated</u> fresh pepper onto the guest's salad.

    A. to cause irritation
    B. a frame of parallel bars
    C. to pulverize by rubbing

_____ 4. As the marathon runner approached the ten-mile marker, he began to <u>tire</u>.

    A. to bore completely
    B. to decrease in physical strength
    C. a solid rubber cushion of a wheel

_____ 5. The plumber gave the woman a <u>bill</u> for repairing the faucet.

    A. list of money owed
    B. the jaws of a bird
    C. a printed advertisement

_____ 6. The quarterback <u>barked</u> the signals loudly to the other players.

    A. to use a short curt sound
    B. to advertise by persistent outcry
    C. the sound made by a dog

_____ 7. The police knew that the witness was a <u>plant</u>.

    A. to fix in place
    B. to establish
    C. to covertly place for discovery

_____ 8. As the surfer paddled into the ocean, she looked intently for the perfect <u>wave</u> to ride.

    A. a rolling movement
    B. a sweep of the hand
    C. to follow a curving line

_____ 9. The hunter thought of the money he would receive for the fine fox <u>pelt</u>.

    A. to beat incessantly
    B. undressed skin
    C. strike with a succession of blows

_____ 10. The boy knew the woman was a nun because of her distinctive <u>habit</u>.

    A. a costume characteristic of a calling
    B. a behavior pattern
    C. a way of acting caused by repetition

PATTERNS OF ERRORS
_____ Inability to understand multiple meaning
    words in context

LEVEL B
Number possible _____ 10 _____
Number correct _____
Accuracy _____

COMMENTS: _____

Comprehension Skills

NAME _____ GRADE __ TEACHER _____

DATE _____ SCHOOL _____

LEVEL C – UNDERSTANDING TECHNICAL WORDS IN CONTEXT

Directions: Read the following sentences carefully. In the blank provided, write the letter of the phrase or word that has the correct meaning for the underlined word. Be sure the meaning chosen is appropriate for the way the word is used in the sentence.

_____ 1. The teacher used the globe to illustrate to the class how the earth rotates on its underline{axis}.

    A. a line indicating the height of an object from its center
    B. a straight line about which a body rotates
    C. the angular elevation of a body

_____ 2. The mapmaker used various colors to illustrate the earth's topography.

    A. configuration of a surface
    B. boundaries of the states
    C. description of a specific section of a map

_____ 3. The Steed family was one of the families who settled in the new colony.

    A. a group of people who leave a country
    B. a body of people living in a new land
    C. a group of people who acquire land by force

_____ 4. The plane flew to the altitude of 20,000 feet before it fired its rockets.

    A. the angular elevation of an object above the horizon
    B. angular distance measured on a great circle
    C. a lengthwise dimension

_____ 5. When the war began, the family decided to emigrate to a new home.

    A. to come to a new country
    B. to establish a new government
    C. to leave a country for a residence elsewhere

_____ 6. Although he knew he would be a traitor, the man decided to sell the top secret documents to the enemy.

    A. a person who commits treason
    B. a person who helps his country grow
    C. a person who is a soldier

_____ 7. The explorers decided to claim the territory for the Queen of England.

    A. large city area
    B. geographical area belonging to a government authority
    C. a body of people living in a designated area

_____ 8. The census bureau claims that fifty <u>per cent</u> of the population lives east of the Mississippi River.

    A. a greater number
    B. the total class or category
    C. a fractional amount of the total

_____ 9. The students in the science class enjoyed studying <u>entomology</u>.

    A. the study of insects
    B. dealing with animals and their environment
    C. causing an infectious disease

_____ 10. The teacher discussed how the object was composed of many <u>molecules</u>.

    A. nucleus of the hydrogen atom
    B. a tiny bit; particle
    C. an uncharged elementary particle

PATTERNS OF ERRORS

_____ Inability to understand technical words
in context

LEVEL C

Number possible   _10_
Number correct   _____
Accuracy   _____

COMMENTS: _____

_____

© 1985 by Parker Publishing Company, Inc.

Comprehension Skills

NAME _____ GRADE ____ TEACHER _____

DATE _____ SCHOOL _____

LEVEL D – RECALLING FACTS READ

Directions: Read carefully the following paragraphs. After you have read each paragraph, answer the questions. Place the letter of the best answer in the blank provided.

A. THE STORM

Weather forecasters warned travelers in the Denver area of a major storm center that was heading toward them. The storm had already deposited fifteen inches of snow on cities in the southwestern portion of the United States, and it seemed to be gaining intensity as it approached Denver. Forecasters feared that the storm would close the airport and all major highways. Travelers were advised to seek shelter and to listen to the weather forecasters on the radio before they attempted to continue their travel. As a precaution, travelers were also requested to notify relatives of where they would be staying and to notify the local authorities if they were involved in an emergency situation.

_____ 1. How many inches of snow were already covering the southwestern section of the United States?
      A. fifteen   C. twenty-five
      B. none

_____ 2. The storm that was heading toward Denver was:
      A. becoming weaker in intensity   C. increasing in intensity
      B. remaining relatively calm

_____ 3. Travelers in the Denver area were advised to seek shelter and to gain information about the storm by:
      A. calling the state police   C. watching television
      B. listening to the radio

B. A NEW LAND

The young voyagers traveled down a long, winding river that was filled with dark murky water. Large reddish birds circled overhead and screeched in an eerie way. Both boys were frightened. They believed that the raft was taking them to a forbidden place, a place where the world was distorted and perhaps somewhat enchanted. Along the shores of the river, one voyager spotted an enormous pincer protruding from the water. The pincer was large enough to grasp the large frog that swam in the water and slice it in half. The animals seemed to have grown beyond their normal size in this environment. They were giants. This place with its strange animal life was indeed enchanted.

_____ 1. The voyagers in the paragraph believed the area that they were exploring was:
    A. beautiful   C. dirty
    B. enchanted

_____ 2. The aquatic life in the river was:
    A. pleasant and enjoyable   C. typical for a river area
    B. oversized and threatening

_____ 3. The voyagers in the paragraph traveled on the river in what type of craft?
    A. canoe   C. raft
    B. motor boat

_____ 4. The voyagers in the paragraph were:
    A. young
    B. adults   C. middle-aged

C. COINS

Coins that you carry around in your pockets are made of combinations of metals rather than of just one metal. The penny, our country's most popular coin, is made of two metals—zinc and copper. Nickels are also made of two metals—nickel and copper. However, in a nickel there is a greater percentage of copper than of nickel. All other coins are made in three layers; they are called composite coins. As there are three layers, all three layers must be bonded together. This process is called "cladding."

_____ 1. The most popular coin in our country is composed of how many metals?
    A. one   C. three
    B. two

_____ 2. What metal is the predominant metal in a nickel?
    A. nickel   C. zinc
    B. copper

_____ 3. The process that bonds three layers of metal to make a coin is called:
    A. bonding   C. cladding
    B. composite

PATTERNS OF ERRORS

_____ Inability to recall facts read

LEVEL D

Number possible   __10__
Number correct   _____
Accuracy   _____

COMMENTS: _____

© 1985 by Parker Publishing Company, Inc.

Comprehension Skills

NAME _____ GRADE ____ TEACHER _____

DATE _____ SCHOOL _____

LEVEL E – FOLLOWING DIRECTIONS READ

Directions: To spell the mystery word, read the directions printed beside each blank. Print the appropriate letter of the alphabet in the blank provided.

A B C D E F G H I J K L M N O P Q R S T U V W X Y Z

1. ____ the fourth letter of the alphabet

2. ____ the third letter to the left of the letter **L**

3. ____ the first letter to the right of the letter **Q**

4. ____ the second letter to the right of the letter **C**

5. ____ the third letter of the alphabet

6. ____ the tenth letter to the right of the letter **J**

7. ____ the fourth letter to the right of the letter **E**

8. ____ the fifteenth letter of the alphabet

9. ____ the fourth letter to the right of the letter **J**

10. ____ the second letter to the left of the letter **U**

The mystery word is _____.

Directions: In each of the following five rows of words, you will find words that name different types of objects. Carefully read and follow the directions which tell you how to mark the words in each row.

Row 1: Circle all the words in the following row that name things that can be driven.

snowmobile   tire   bumper   truck

Row 2: Circle all the words in the following row that name foods.

taco   poison ivy   cement   peanuts

Row 3: Circle all the words in the following row that name things that can be worn.

apron   tree   scarf   orange

Row 4: Circle all the words in the following row that name toys.

ball   doll   hat   shoe

Row 5: Circle all the words in the following row that name things that are not grown.

grapes   dish   knife   squash

PATTERNS OF ERRORS

_____ Inability to follow directions read

LEVEL E

Number possible   20
Number correct   _____
Accuracy   _____

COMMENTS: _____

© 1985 by Parker Publishing Company, Inc.

Comprehension Skills

NAME _____ GRADE __ TEACHER _____

DATE _____ SCHOOL _____

LEVEL F – SEQUENCING IDEAS READ

Directions: Study each of the following number or letter sequences. Determine what combination of numbers or letters should be written in the blank at the end of the line to correctly complete the sequence. Write the appropriate letters or numbers in the blank.

1. 1,3,5; 2,4,6; 7,9,11; _____.

2. A, BB, CCC, _____.

3. STEVE, EVETS, PAT, _____.

4. 2+3, 3+5, 5+8, _____.

5. AZ, BY, CX, _____.

Directions: Study the sentences listed below. Determine the proper sequence of events. Number the events in their proper sequence from 1 to 5.

_____ Cut the tree trunk into logs.

_____ Place the logs in the fireplace.

_____ Locate a fallen tree trunk.

_____ Roast marshmallows.

_____ Light the fire.

_____

PATTERNS OF ERRORS

_____ Inability to sequence ideas read

LEVEL F

Number possible __10__
Number correct _____
Accuracy   _____

COMMENTS: _____

_____

Comprehension Skills

NAME _____ GRADE ____ TEACHER_____

DATE _____ SCHOOL _____

LEVEL G – SELECTING IMPORTANT DETAILS

Directions: Read carefully the following paragraphs. After you have read each paragraph, select the correct answer for each question. Place the letter of the correct answer in the blank provided.

A. THE BLACK STALLION

The black stallion was an imposing figure to the boy. The horse was almost sixteen hands high at the shoulder and seemed to dwarf the young boy who stood at his side. As the boy reached upward and stroked the horse's massive chest, he could feel the enormous muscles that lay just beneath the skin. The horse's chest was deep and powerful, a mark of a true Arabian stallion. As they walked beside the race track, the boy wondered if the horse could indeed run as fast as the famous horse Man O' War. A horse that could run like this black stallion certainly must be capable of racing. However, there was the question of the horse's high spirit. Could the boy control the stallion and make him run or would the stallion choose to fight with the other horses? Although the boy wished to ride the horse and test his ability, he would heed his uncle's words and continue to merely exercise the horse in the paddock area. He would have to wait until tomorrow before this fine animal could run on the track.

_____ 1. What breed of horse was the black stallion?

    A. black
    B. Arabian
    C. race horse

_____ 2. What was the setting for this paragraph?

    A. a farm
    B. a rodeo
    C. a race track

_____ 3. Why was the boy waiting until tomorrow to let the horse run?

    A. The horse was injured.
    B. The horse's spirit was too high.
    C. The boy was obeying his uncle.

B. THE KILLER

As the police cruiser sped toward the department store, the officer inside could not help wondering whether or not the witnesses to the crime could give him specific details about the killer. In particular, he would need to have the person's approximate height and weight. He would also need to know the person's race and the color of his hair and eyes. Perhaps the most important part of the description, and the one detail that probably would lead to the killer's arrest, was whether or not there were any distinguishing marks on his face and/or body. The officer was particularly hopeful that someone had noticed an unusual characteristic. However, from his previous experiences with witnesses to a crime, he had found that they were usually too stunned by the crime to note many specific details about the killer. He was hopeful, however, that perhaps this time the witnesses would be of more help.

_____ 1. The main character in the paragraph was:

    A. the killer
    B. the witness
    C. the police officer

_____ 2. Why were the witnesses to a crime usually of little help in identifying the killer?

    A. They were not paying attention when the crime occurred.
    B. They were usually too stunned by the crime.
    C. The killer usually threatened to kill them if they talked to the police.

_____ 3. The main detail that would probably aid in the arrest of the killer was:

    A. distinguishing marks on his face and/or body
    B. his hair color
    C. his height and weight

_____ 4. The man in the paragraph proceeded toward the scene of the crime in what type of vehicle?

    A. a motorcycle
    B. a car
    C. an ambulance

C. THE TENNIS PLAYER

Professional tennis players must prepare themselves in many ways when they are playing in a tournament. Perhaps one of the most critical aspects of their preparation is physical conditioning. To be in top physical condition, they must jog at least ten miles a day and practice for four or more hours a day. During the practice sessions, each stroke must be perfected so that their opponents will not be able to exploit any weakness in their game. A professional tennis player spends a designated amount of time, usually twenty minutes, on each stroke. If he has a particular stroke, such as the overhead smash, which is weak, he will spend extra time perfecting that shot. Being a professional tennis player is a very demanding occupation.

_____ 1. Professional tennis players prepare for a tournament in many ways. Perhaps the most important part of their preparation is:

    A. serving
    B. physical conditioning
    C. mental ability

_____ 2. How far should a professional tennis player jog in one day?

    A. 20 miles
    B. less than 5 miles
    C. at least 10 miles

_____ 3. Why do tennis players spend many long hours practicing?

    A. because of their coaches
    B. so they have no weak strokes
    C. so their overhead smash is strong

PATTERNS OF ERRORS

_____ Inability to select important details

LEVEL G

Number possible __10__
Number correct _____
Accuracy _____

COMMENTS: _____

Comprehension Skills

NAME _____ GRADE ____ TEACHER _____

DATE _____ SCHOOL _____

LEVEL H – IDENTIFYING MAIN IDEAS NOT EXPLICITLY STATED

Directions: Read each paragraph below. Using the list of suggested titles, determine the best title or subject area for each paragraph. Write the appropriate letter of the answer in the blank beside the paragraph. Use each answer only once. You will have some titles that you will not use.

TITLES

A. Playing Tennis
B. Learning to Ski
C. Playing Badminton
D. Playing Soccer
E. The Coming of Spring
F. The Coming of Summer
G. The Coming of Autumn
H. The Beginning of Winter

I. Raking Leaves
J. Cutting the Grass
K. The Library
L. The Grocery Store
M. The Hardware Store
N. Annapolis Naval Academy
O. West Point Military Academy

_____ 1. As the family car climbed higher up the mountain, the children spied the first hint of the coming season. Far to the right of the car, a few of the leaves on the sugar maple tree had turned a dark crimson red. With the cool nights, the leaves would now quickly turn until the mountain would soon be aglow with color.

_____ 2. As mother ushered the children through the automatic door, they raced forward to see which one of them would ride in the cart. Mother busily sifted through the jumbled contents of her purse until she spotted her lengthy list of items that she had come to purchase. Judging by the length of the list, the children knew that it would be quite a while before all the cans, bags, bunches, and cartons of products were in the deep, basketlike center of the cart, and they could proceed to the checkout line.

_____ 3. Dana entered the large double doors and stepped quietly up to the large desk that stood between the many long columns of books and large tables. Perhaps the woman behind the desk would direct her to the proper reference area for getting information on her report topic. For her last report she had begun her research at the card catalog file, but since this report was about the effects of cigarette smoking, she thought the vertical file would be a more appropriate place to do her research.

TITLES

A. Playing Tennis
B. Learning to Ski
C. Playing Badminton
D. Playing Soccer
E. The Coming of Spring
F. The Coming of Summer
G. The Coming of Autumn
H. The Beginning of Winter

I. Raking Leaves
J. Cutting the Grass
K. The Library
L. The Grocery Store
M. The Hardware Store
N. Annapolis Naval Academy
O. West Point Military Academy

_____ 4. Charlie had looked forward all day to this class period. He had anticipated the game, and he had dressed in jeans and tennis shoes. However, he was not sure what game they would be playing today. Although the ball was round, it was painted so that several sections were of one color. Charlie also noticed that the two goals were positioned so that one was at either end of the field. In front of each goal stood a boy; he was the goaltender and his job was to block the ball before it entered the goal. Charlie hoped that he would have a chance to be goaltender.

_____ 5. The picnic was great fun and the food was delicious, particularly the charcoaled hot dogs. However, Nancy did not like the flies and bugs which were encircling her food. Although she enjoyed this season of the year and eagerly anticipated her first dive into the nearby swimming pool, she had been sad yesterday to see school end.

_____ 6. It was slip and slide today as the first heavy snow of the season fell on the city. Most motorists were stranded by the surprise snowfall, and they spent many hours attempting to drive home. To try to ease the traffic congestion that resulted, salt trucks and their crews were now on the highways.

_____ 7. As Michael read the travel brochure, he was extremely interested in the advertisement for Maryland. "Come to Maryland," said the brochure, "and visit this interesting educational facility. Most of the country's naval officers have graduated from this school, and some graduates such as Roger Stauback have gained national prominence. Students wishing to attend this school must enjoy sailing and working aboard a ship."

_____ 8. Steve hated the thought of dragging out the machine. He did not hate the machine itself, but rather the chore it helped him complete. He had known for a long time that weeds, grass, and dust made him sneeze. As soon as he began to push the machine through the yard, he was sure he would again be coughing and sneezing. As the machine lurched forward, he remembered that he would also need to take a rake to gather the excess debris that would be left.

TITLES

A. Playing Tennis
B. Learning to Ski
C. Playing Badminton
D. Playing Soccer
E. The Coming of Spring
F. The Coming of Summer
G. The Coming of Autumn
H. The Beginning of Winter

I. Raking Leaves
J. Cutting the Grass
K. The Library
L. The Grocery Store
M. The Hardware Store
N. Annapolis Naval Academy
O. West Point Military Academy

_____ 9. Mary swatted viciously at the low-flying birdie. She had never liked to play this game. Not only did she have trouble swinging the racquet so that it would strike the birdie and send it over the net, but she also had trouble keeping the birdie in bounds after she had hit it. However, since this was a picnic and the other players seemed to enjoy the game, she would do her best to help her side to win.

_____ 10. Jacques stood at the top of the cold, snow-covered slope, and marveled at the skill with which his friends stood on the long laminated boards attached to their feet and gracefully guided them down the slope. He only hoped that the poles which he held in his hands would slow his rate of speed and help him to avoid the many pine trees that dotted the slope below.

PATTERNS OF ERRORS
_____ Inability to identify main ideas not
    explicitly stated

LEVEL H
Number possible   _10_
Number correct   _____
Accuracy   _____

COMMENTS: _____

Comprehension Skills

NAME _____ GRADE ____ TEACHER _____

DATE _____ SCHOOL _____

LEVEL I – DRAWING LOGICAL CONCLUSIONS

Directions: Read each of the following paragraphs and answer the question that follows. Place the letter of the correct answer in the blank provided.

_____ 1. As the man studied the wind gauge on the outside of the building, he became increasingly alarmed. The winds on this tropical island were becoming stronger. He anxiously looked at the barometer and the rain gauge and found that the air pressure was falling while the rain was increasing in intensity.

What was the weatherman afraid was happening?

A. A hurricane was coming.
B. An earthquake was taking place.
C. A snowstorm was approaching.

_____ 2. Intently the pilot watched the gauges on his plane's instrument panel. He noticed that they were rapidly losing altitude and that the plane's right engine was no longer functioning. As he glanced over his shoulder, he noticed that the copilot was urgently sending a message about their current position.

What was happening to the plane?

A. The plane was preparing to land at the airport.
B. The plane was going to crash.
C. The plane was conducting a series of practice maneuvers.

_____ 3. The baby sat near the Christmas poinsettia and studied the plant's bright red leaves. As she did, a tiny, berry-like object fell from the plant. Before the baby's mother could pick up the fallen object, the child had placed it in her mouth and swallowed it. Her mother became frantic because she knew that parts of the poinsettia plant are poisonous. She raced to the telephone and dialed the number of the agency that she knew could help her.

Whom was the mother calling?

A. the local fire department
B. the local school
C. the local hospital

_____ 4. The football game had remained tied for the last two quarters and now time was running out. Only five seconds remained on the game clock. As the quarterback dropped back to pass, he saw the end cut into the center of the end zone. As the defensive lineman crashed into him, he passed the ball in the direction of the end. As he lay on the ground, the quarterback could hear his hometown crowd yelling and screaming in delight.

What had happened?

A. The quarterback's team had won the game.
B. The crowd was pleased because the quarterback was hit.
C. The end had dropped the ball.

_____ 5. The two men sat in the cockpit at the top of the enormous rocket. Before this mission, neither one of them had ever been in space. As they listened to the countdown which would signal the exact moment when their craft would be sent speeding into space, they wondered what value rocks from the moon would be to the earth's future.

Who were these men?

A. aliens
B. robots
C. modern explorers

_____ 6. One species of prehistoric cat would not have made a good pet. His two front teeth were extremely long. When he attacked an animal, he would sink these two saber-like teeth into the animal to kill him. After the animal was dead, the cat would then use the teeth to slice the animal into pieces.

What was this prehistoric cat?

A. a mastodon
B. a saber-toothed tiger
C. Tyrannosaurus Rex

_____ 7. John wondered why the metal object in his front yard was shaped as it was. With its three protruding metal arms and its silly-looking pointed top, it looked almost like a person. In fact, in some towns people had painted faces on these objects. However, aside from its strange looks, John knew that its most important function was in case of a fire. Firemen would attach hoses to it and release water to fight the fire.

What is this strange object?

A. a mailbox
B. a fireplug
C. a water faucet

_____ 8. The man seated behind the large elevated wooden desk was listening intently as the lawyer presented his opening arguments. Off to the side the jury sat in silence, for they were attempting to determine whether this man should live or die.

Where were these people?

A. at school
B. at a police station
C. in a courtroom

_____ 9. There are three distinct types of these white puffy substances: (1) cirrus, (2) stratus, and (3) cumulus. Each of the three types is quite different. Cirrus are found high in the sky and are made up of tiny ice crystals. Stratus are found at about 2,000 feet and carry rain or snow. Cumulus are big and scattered and appear when we have fine weather.

What are these substances?
A. stars
B. clouds
C. wind currents

_____ 10. As David crouched in the starting blocks, he listened intently for the sound of the starter's pistol. The loud sound of the pistol set him and the other runners off toward the numerous hurdles that lay before them. As he approached the first hurdle, David was taxing every muscle in his body. He knew he was gaining on the leader. David sprinted past the leader and leaped over the final hurdle.

How did the race end?

A. The two boys crossed the finish line at the same time.
B. David won the race.
C. David lost the race.

1985 by Parker Publishing Company, Inc.

PATTERNS OF ERRORS
_____ Inability to draw logical conclusions

LEVEL I
Number possible _10_
Number correct _____
Accuracy _____

COMMENTS: _____

Comprehension Skills

NAME _____ GRADE __ TEACHER _____

DATE _____ SCHOOL _____

LEVEL J – PREDICTING LOGICAL OUTCOMES

Directions: Read each of the following paragraphs and answer the questions that appear at the end of the paragraphs. Write your answers in the space provided.

A. As the people looked upward at the darkening sky, they could feel the increasing intensity of the wind. They had already had rain for two straight days. Rains that were intense and heavy like these always caused the rivers and streams to rise above their banks. As they frantically piled sandbags beside the now rampaging river, they could not help wondering what new damage the impending rains would bring.

What do you believe the rains will cause to happen? Give three answers.

1. _____

_____

2. _____

_____

3. _____

_____

B. William wondered what service a ten-year-old boy could be to his country in these troubled colonial times. As he sat listening to his father that evening, he realized that he could probably be of great service to General Sumter. His father had said that the British Army had sealed off all exits from the South Carolina island, and there was apparently no way to get a message to General Greene. William hesitantly approached his father and explained to him that he could go through the great swamp and successfully reach General Greene. His journey would take approximately two days, but William was certain that he could travel through the swamp safely.

If you were William, what four items would you take with you on your journey?

1. _____   2. _____

3. _____   4. _____

C. Regina always enjoyed shopping with her mother in the huge indoor shopping mall. It was exciting to be among all the people and to explore the bright little shops that were housed in the mall. She had been intently studying a toy in a shop when she suddenly realized that her mother was not nearby. Believing that her mother was in another part of the small shop, Regina hastily searched up and down each aisle. To her surprise, her mother was gone and Regina realized that she was lost.

List three actions that Regina could take to try to find her mother.

1. _____

_____

2. _____

_____

3. _____

_____

_____

_____

PATTERNS OF ERRORS

_____ Inability to predict logical outcomes

LEVEL J

Number possible __10__
Number correct ____
Accuracy ____

COMMENTS: _____

_____

© 1985 by Parker Publishing Company, Inc.

Comprehension Skills

NAME _____ GRADE _____ TEACHER _____

DATE _____ SCHOOL _____

LEVEL K – INTERPRETING KEY CONCEPTS ABOUT STORY CHARACTERS

Directions: Read each of the following paragraphs. Determine the best answer for the questions. Write the letter of the correct answer in the blank provided.

A. THE GATE

The nervous little man walked briskly through the airplane terminal and tentatively approached the security gate. He had spent many hours devising a plan to smuggle the stolen jewelry past the security guard. As the bag with the concealed jewelry passed down the conveyor belt toward the surveillance equipment, he squirmed nervously, and anxiously shifted his eyes from the bag to the burly security guard who stood beside the gate.

The guard had been watching the man as he approached the gate, and wondered why this man was so nervous. In his very deliberate manner, the guard began to silently review all the possibilities that could cause this man to be so nervous. Because of his training at the academy, he was instinctively aware of a person's mannerisms. He paid particular attention to the eyes of the persons who passed through the gate. Although in rare instances the equipment did not detect a hidden substance, people's mannerisms often betrayed their dishonest ventures and caused them to be caught.

_____ 1. Which character in the story would be more likely to notice a distinctive mannerism in a person?

    A. the thief
    B. the guard

_____ 2. What words would you select to describe the guard?

    A. large, fat, nervous
    B. heavy, observant, systematic
    C. strong, well-trained, good-natured

_____ 3. If the thief were caught by the guard, what two things (other than the surveillance equipment) do you think would lead to his capture?

    A. rapid walk and short stature
    B. nervous mannerisms and shifty eyes
    C. size of the bag and the manner in which he spoke

B. MATT DILLON—SHERIFF

The frontier saloon was crowded with people on this hot summer day. Many people in the territory had come to Dodge City to celebrate the election of Matt Dillon as sheriff. Mr. Dillon was a soft-spoken man who was a skilled leader and frontiersman. He was not like the drunken Doc Holiday, who spent most of his days drinking himself into a stupor. Although Matt and Doc were the same age, they were exceedingly different in stature and demeanor. However, they did have one characteristic in common: both were exceptionally fast with their guns. This fact alone seemed to be why the men were friends. Both were also concerned with restoring justice to this land and ridding it of outlaws like the Dalton Gang. According to Festus, Matt's new deputy, the members of the gang were no good, conniving culprits. Of course, Festus did like to overdramatize anything that he discussed. The Daltons, who lived in an isolated section of the Badlands, were commonly known to be outlaws. They were notorious these days for the many banks they had robbed and the people they had killed. It was also common knowledge that they had recently robbed the bank in the neighboring town and, if Festus could be believed, shot the banker and his wife. Matt believed that the Daltons were certain to come to Dodge City and confront him, Festus, and Doc. The outcome of such a confrontation was debated openly by the town's people, and their strong feelings had led them to elect Matt Dillon as their sheriff.

_____ 1. Although Festus was a likable fellow, everyone in Dodge City knew that he:

    A. spent too much time at the saloon
    B. liked to exaggerate the truth
    C. was a friend of the Daltons

_____ 2. Which one of the characters described in the story would be described as courageous, fearless, and resourceful?

    A. Matt Dillon
    B. Festus
    C. Doc Holiday

_____ 3. If you were to characterize the Dalton Gang, what words would you choose?

    A. cunning, notorious
    B. remorseful, sympathetic
    C. drunken, stupid

C. THE POT OF GOLD

As the young boy stooped to retrieve the ball which had become lodged in the small space between the jagged rocks, he was surprised to be greeted by a tiny elfin creature. This jovial creature asked the boy if he would like to see the pot of gold at the end of the rainbow. The boy was quite stunned and looked at the elf in disbelief.

"Sure!" the boy said aloud. "I would be glad to accompany you to the gold."

As the elf gaily skipped over the nearest boulder, he asked, "Will you vow to leave the gold where it is and never disclose its location to anyone?"

"Yes," said the boy eagerly.

"Then follow me," the elf replied.

Off they went through the forest toward the rainbow. As the boy followed anxiously along behind the elf, he thought of the many things he would do with all the gold he was about to acquire. His mind raced at the thought of it. His promise to the elf was of no value, he thought to himself, for he had often lied to his parents and friends.

The elf was very wise, and he led the boy over the most treacherous and difficult paths he could find. He wanted to be certain that this boy was trustworthy, and the long trip would give him the opportunity to evaluate the boy.

"Why are you willing to follow me to the gold when you know that you cannot take any of it with you?" asked the elf.

The boy cautiously replied, "I have never seen a large amount of gold and I would just like to see how much it glows."

The elf laughed as he raced over the rocks for he knew by the tone of the boy's voice that he was lying.

_____ 1. From the words listed below, select two words that best describe the boy in the story and write the letters of the two correct answers in the blank provided.

    A. loving
    B. clever
    C. cunning
    D. untrustworthy

_____ 2. From the words listed below, select two words that best describe the elf in the story and write the letters of the two correct answers in the blank provided.

    A. clever
    B. mean
    C. happy
    D. treacherous

PATTERNS OF ERRORS

_____ Inability to interpret key concepts
about story characters

LEVEL K

Number possible   _10_
Number correct   _____
Accuracy   _____

COMMENTS: _____

Comprehension Skills

NAME _____ GRADE ____ TEACHER _____

DATE _____ SCHOOL _____

LEVEL L – ASSOCIATING THE TEXT WITH THE CORRECT PICTURE

Directions: Study the illustrations on page 83 and read the brief paragraphs below. All of the paragraphs are about famous people, and the illustrations depict an important part of their lives. Match each paragraph with the correct picture. Write the letter of the correct picture on the blank beside each paragraph.

_____ 1. Noah Webster was born in Connecticut in 1758. Webster was a schoolteacher who wrote the first dictionary.

_____ 2. Orville Wright was born in 1871 in Dayton, Ohio. Along with his brother Wilbur, he invented the airplane. Their first plane made its first successful flight on December 17, 1903, at Kitty Hawk, North Carolina.

_____ 3. William R. Anderson and a crew of 116 men sailed the submarine, Nautilus, beneath the Polar ice cap. They made history by sailing father north than any other ship.

_____ 4. Paul Revere was born in Massachusetts in 1735. In 1775 he rode through the streets of Boston and warned the people of the advancing British troops.

_____ 5. Ferdinand Magellan was born in Portugal in about 1480. He was the first sea captain to discover a water passage in South America that linked the Atlantic Ocean to the Pacific Ocean.

_____ 6. Thomas Alva Edison was born in 1847. In 1879 he invented the first light bulb. It burned for more than 40 hours.

_____ 7. Henry Ford was born in 1863 in Michigan. In the 1900s he wanted to produce a car that cost less than $500. The car that he produced was the Model T.

_____ 8. Eli Whitney was born in 1765 in Massachusetts. He later invented the cotton gin, a machine that pulled the seeds out of the cotton.

_____ 9. Leif Ericsson, the Viking, was the discoverer of the New World. He sailed in a single-masted Viking boat that had a red mouth and the green eyes of a snake painted on its bow.

_____ 10. Benjamin Franklin was born in Boston in 1706. Franklin had many talents and he invented many things. One of his inventions, the lightning rod, enabled man to avoid the disastrous effect of lightning.

© 1985 by Parker Publishing Company, Inc.

PATTERNS OF ERRORS
_____ Inability to associate the text with
the correct picture

LEVEL L
Number possible ___10___
Number correct _____
Accuracy _____

COMMENTS: _____

A.

B.

C.

D.

E.

F.

G.

H.

I.

J.

Comprehension Skills

NAME _____ GRADE __ TEACHER _____

DATE _____ SCHOOL _____

LEVEL M – FOLLOWING PLOT SEQUENCE

Directions: Below are four lists of events that would take place in a particular sequence if you were using them to write a story. Place a number (1, 2, 3, 4, or 5) in the blank beside each sentence to show the order in which you would use each event when writing a story.

List 1

____ A. Nancy wraps the present for the birthday party.

____ B. Nancy eats cake and ice cream at the party.

____ C. Nancy receives an invitation to Kelly's birthday party.

____ D. Nancy selects a present to take to Kelly's birthday party.

____ E. Nancy and the other children sing "Happy Birthday" to Kelly.

List 2

____ A. The family goes to the beach to swim.

____ B. The family travels on the highway.

____ C. The family arrives at the resort motel.

____ D. The family packs the luggage for the trip.

____ E. The family celebrates the last day of school.

List 3

____ A. Steve rehearses with the school orchestra.

____ B. Steve and the orchestra bow as the audience applauds.

____ C. Steve is selected to play in the school orchestra.

____ D. Steve and the orchestra leave the concert stage.

____ E. Steve and the orchestra play in the concert.

List 4

____ A. Chris and his father decide to go fishing.

____ B. Chris feeds the fish to the cats.

____ C. Chris and his father load the fishing equipment into the boat.

____ D. Chris catches an 18-inch bass.

____ E. Chris's father rows the boat out from shore.

PATTERNS OF ERRORS

____ Inability to follow plot sequence

LEVEL M

Number possible __20__

Number correct ____

Accuracy ____

COMMENTS: _____

Comprehension Skills

NAME _____ GRADE __ TEACHER _____

DATE _____ SCHOOL _____

LEVEL N – CLASSIFYING INFORMATION

Directions: Study the words listed below. Write each of the words under its appropriate subject area.

latitude	Uranus	orbit
biology	climate	column
addend	equals	punctuate
sentence	adverb	disaster
tens	capitalization	experiment
paragraph	molecules	addition
explore	irrigation	

SOCIAL STUDIES	SCIENCE	ARITHMETIC	ENGLISH
_____	_____	_____	_____
_____	_____	_____	_____
_____	_____	_____	_____
_____	_____	_____	_____
_____	_____	_____	_____

_____

_____

PATTERNS OF ERRORS   LEVEL N

____ Inability to classify information   Number possible _20_
                                              Number correct   ____
                                              Accuracy   ____

COMMENTS: _____

_____

Comprehension Skills

NAME _____ GRADE __ TEACHER _____

DATE _____ SCHOOL _____

LEVEL O – DETERMINING CAUSE-AND-EFFECT RELATIONSHIPS

Directions: Study the two lists given below: on the left is a list of <u>cause</u> statements and on the right a list of <u>effect</u> statements. Match each <u>cause</u> in the left column with the <u>effect</u> that would result. Place the letter of the correct answer in the blank provided.

<table>
<tr><td colspan="2"><u>CAUSES</u></td><td><u>EFFECTS</u></td></tr>
<tr><td>____</td><td>1. Rains deluge the town.</td><td>A. Repairman is called.</td></tr>
<tr><td>____</td><td>2. Boy breaks arm in fall.</td><td>B. Cars unable to travel on roads.</td></tr>
<tr><td>____</td><td>3. Child's toe rubs front of her shoe.</td><td>C. Many homes flooded.</td></tr>
<tr><td>____</td><td>4. Temperatures in the 100 degree range.</td><td>D. Dog wins obedience trophy at dog show.</td></tr>
<tr><td>____</td><td>5. Woman eats three candy bars a day.</td><td>E. Plans to go on diet are made.</td></tr>
<tr><td>____</td><td>6. Girl returns overdue book to library.</td><td>F. Students miss first period class.</td></tr>
<tr><td>____</td><td>7. School bus arrives at school one hour late.</td><td>G. Doctor places cast on arm.</td></tr>
<tr><td>____</td><td>8. Early morning snowstorm buries town.</td><td>H. Swimming pools are crowded.</td></tr>
<tr><td>____</td><td>9. Television does not work.</td><td>I. Student pays library fine.</td></tr>
<tr><td>____</td><td>10. Dog and master attend obedience classes.</td><td>J. New shoes are purchased at store.</td></tr>
</table>

Directions: Circle the word or words in the following sentences that alert you that a cause or reason is being stated.

1. I do not win many tennis matches because I do not practice.
2. Because Mary watched television late into the evening, she did not awaken early enough to catch the school bus.
3. Mike is very strong; for this reason, everyone thinks he plays for the football team.
4. Harry lost his credit card, and consequently, he is unable to buy the sweater on credit.
5. I ate continuously over the holidays; therefore, I gained ten additional pounds.

PATTERNS OF ERRORS	LEVEL O
____ Inability to determine cause and effect relationships	Number possible __15__
	Number correct ____
	Accuracy ____

COMMENTS: _____

Comprehension Skills

NAME _____ GRADE ____ TEACHER _____

DATE _____ SCHOOL _____

LEVEL P – SUMMARIZING MATERIAL READ—PART I

Directions: Each of the summary statements listed below can be used to summarize the events or actions described in one of the paragraphs that follow. Read each of the paragraphs and identify the event or action that is being described. Match each of the summary statements with the appropriate paragraph. Write the letter of the correct summary statement in the blank provided.

SUMMARY STATEMENTS

A. What would you find in a big city?
B. Events leading to the Civil War.
C. An evening at the ballet.
D. The family prepares for Christmas Day.
E. A safety check for your automobile.

____ 1. —The family arrives at the tree nursery and chooses a pine tree.
—The ornaments used to decorate the tree are unpacked.
—The family places lights, tinsel, and ornaments on the tree.
—The family places gifts under the tree.

____ 2. —Abraham Lincoln serves as President of the United States.
—People who live in the northern states object to the use of slavery on southern plantations.
—Fort Sumter is attacked on April 12, 1861.
—The South chooses General Robert E. Lee to lead its troops.
—The North chooses Ulysses S. Grant to lead its troops.

____ 3. —The orchestra arrives at the theatre and begins to tune up for the performance.
—The audience filters into the theatre and quickly finds their seats.
—The dancers complete the final act of their performance.
—The dancers retire to their dressing rooms and begin to remove their makeup.

____ 4. —The mechanic checks the car's tires, lights, windshield wipers, and exhaust system.
—All defective parts of the car are replaced with new parts.
—The car is taken for a test drive by the mechanic before it is returned to its owner.
—The mechanic places a current safety sticker on the car's windshield.

____ 5. —Forty-story buildings tower overhead.
—Major companies have their offices in many of the skyscrapers.
—Mass transit systems shuttle people from place to place.
—Thousands of people who do not use the mass transit system are caught in the morning rush hour traffic.

LEVEL P – SUMMARIZING MATERIAL READ—PART II

Directions: Read the following paragraphs and match them with one of the three summary statements that follow each. Write the letter of the correct summary statement in the blank provided.

_____ 1. Mike awakened from a night of rest and briskly walked to the bathroom. As he reached for his razor, Mike also reached for a cigarette, the first cigarette of many that he would smoke during the day. Since his twentieth birthday, Mike had been smoking three packs of cigarettes per day. He had also been overeating at mealtime and snacking on sweets between meals. A lack of exercise had also been a pattern in Mike's life for these past ten years. As he began to shave, Mike contemplated the plump face that stared back at him from the mirror. He was, he thought, a prime candidate for a heart attack.

A. The evil effects of smoking
B. Twenty is a crucial age for heart attack patients
C. Factors that can contribute to a heart attack

_____ 2. As Bill sat in the army hut and intently stared at the radar screen, he thought that he was indeed fortunate to have been assigned to the island of Hawaii. Little did he or any of the other servicemen stationed on the island realize that in two hours the island paradise would be transformed into a battle zone. The battle would last but a short time; however, it would draw the United States into a worldwide conflict. Perhaps the most frustrating part of the day for Bill would be his urgent pleas to his superiors to prepare for the attacking Japanese planes— planes which he alone would see on his radar screen and planes which no one on the island would believe were approaching. Although Bill would give the fleet advance warning of the attack, no one would believe that his radar sightings were correct.

A. The peaceful island paradise of Hawaii
B. Japanese planes attack an unsuspecting American base in the Pacific
C. A radar man saves the day and the fleet stationed in the harbor

_____ 3. The young man had first seen the spaniel pup when it was four weeks old. From that day until he took it home three weeks later, the man had been reading about how to train the dog. When he brought the dog home, he was determined that it would become a great obedience champion. When the dog was six months old, the man worked slowly with the young dog and taught it to respond to the word "No" and to come when called—lessons the man knew would be important in acquainting the dog with various other commands. Throughout the next six weeks, the man would spend thirty minutes a day training the dog to sit, stay, heel, and retrieve. Training a dog was tedious and demanding, but the man knew that all of his hard work would not go unrewarded. The dog was intelligent, and the man was certain the spaniel would one day become an obedience champion.

A. Choosing a champion dog is a difficult task
B. Obedience work is tedious and tiring work
C. A dog can be an obedience champion if he is carefully trained

_____ 4. There was an eerie feeling associated with this old home. The many families who had lived here over the past ten years had never stayed longer than two years. Most of the families had left quite suddenly, claiming that the house was haunted. Its old floors were said to creak loudly during the night and strange happenings were said to occur frequently. Consequently, Mary was very frightened as she lay in her bed and heard the clank, clank, clank of chains being dragged through the hallway outside her bedroom. Her mind raced as she envisioned a grotesque creature lurking outside her bedroom door—a door which was now opening very slowly. Mary stared into the darkness and strained to see who or what was entering her room.

A. A young girl's desire to become a great detective
B. Strange events that occurred in the basement of a haunted house
C. A frightening experience in an old house

_____ 5. Jack had searched the ground for many hours, and his efforts had been richly rewarded. By carefully sifting through the dirt and mud, he had discovered some articles from a past civilization. Most of the items were clay pots, cups, or flint arrowheads. Some of the artifacts were round, some were triangular, and some (unfortunately) were broken. Jack eagerly collected his newfound treasures and carefully placed them into a large box that he had brought along with him for this purpose. He was anxious to get home and study the items further. Jack planned to take those items which were in excellent condition to the Museum of Natural History. Perhaps the scientists could study the artifacts and tell Jack about the early civilization that had used them.

A. How civilizations had lived in early America
B. A young explorer discovers relics from the past
C. How a Natural History Museum studies early civilizations

© 1985 by Parker Publishing Company, Inc.

PATTERNS OF ERRORS

_____ Inability to summarize material read

LEVEL P
PARTS I AND II
Number possible __10__
Number correct _____
Accuracy _____

COMMENTS: _____

Comprehension Skills

LEVEL Q – IDENTIFYING AND UNDERSTANDING FIGURES OF
        SPEECH—PART I

Directions: Match the definitions on the right with the correct figure of speech
listed on the left. Place the letter of the correct definition in the blank
beside the correct figure of speech.

FIGURES OF SPEECH	DEFINITIONS
____ 1. personification	A. short, local expressions
____ 2. simile	B. giving human qualities to an object that is not human
____ 3. metaphor	C. an implied comparison of two unlike objects
____ 4. idioms	D. substitution of an agreeable expression for an offensive one
____ 5. euphemism	E. comparison of two unlike objects using the words like, as, or than

LEVEL Q – IDENTIFYING AND UNDERSTANDING FIGURES OF
        SPEECH—PART II

Directions: Match the figures of speech listed below with the sentences that
follow. Place the letter of the appropriate figure of speech (A, B, or C)
in the blank beside the sentence which illustrates that figure of
speech. You will use each figure of speech more than once.

A. Personification
B. Simile
C. Metaphor

____ 1. The little boy was as clumsy as a bull in a china shop.
____ 2. Winter's icy fingers grasped the morning.
____ 3. The sun was a river of light.
____ 4. The lion was king of the jungle.
____ 5. In the July heat, the room was like an oven.
____ 6. The kind woman had a heart of gold.
____ 7. The breeze whispered through the forest.
____ 8. As the grandmother listened to the children playing, their laughter was music to her ears.
____ 9. The frightened woman was as white as a ghost.
____ 10. The sun embraced the morning dew.

PATTERNS OF ERRORS

____ Inability to identify and understand
figures of speech

LEVEL Q
PARTS I AND II
Number possible ___15_
Number correct ____
Accuracy ____

COMMENTS: _____

Comprehension Skills

NAME _____ GRADE __ TEACHER _____

DATE _____ SCHOOL _____

LEVEL R – DETECTING AND INTERPRETING PROPAGANDA
          TECHNIQUES

Directions: Match the propaganda techniques listed below with the statements
that follow. Place the letter of the appropriate propaganda technique
in the blank provided beside each statement. You will use each
answer more than once.

A. Testimonial
B. Glittering generalities
C. Bandwagon
D. Emotionally charged words
E. Plain folk talk
F. Transfer technique

_____ 1. Hi! I'm Jack Strongarm and I play for the California Bears
Football Team. I have been using Magnificent Toothpaste
for the past three years and my teeth are in excellent condition.

_____ 2. I have found my boss to be a time-wasting, dictatorial person who is insensitive to his employees' needs.

_____ 3. Many people in the past two years have switched to
"Stretch Socks." Why don't you join them!

_____ 4. My name is Justice P. Pupil, and I am a student just like
you. Vote for me in the coming senior class elections, and
you can be sure that I'll represent you fairly.

_____ 5. When doing your grocery shopping, be sure to choose Super
Soft Cereal. You'll like its better taste.

_____ 6. Are you bored with the same old job? Would you like to be
the leader of your company and not just an employee? Try
Executive Hair Spray. Executive is the newest, most exciting hair spray ever produced by the Dynamite Company. It
can make you the executive you deserve to be. Try it today!

_____ 7. Tired of dull, gray-looking clothes? Use Suds. When you use
Suds in your washing machine, you will have whiter-look-
ing clothes.

_____ 8. Ride the bus today. All your friends and important people
in your company ride the bus to work. Why don't you join
them tomorrow!

_____ 9. Are you driving the car you deserve to drive? Drive the car
that Joe Athlete drives. Joe says, "This car will make you
feel like a super athlete. Drive it today!"

_____ 10. Buy the new "Hot Seat." It provides the natural orthopedic cushioning and therapeutic warmth that your body craves.

_____ 11. You cannot afford to pass up this remarkable film offer. If you are as intelligent as the thousands of people who use our products, you will switch to Quicko Film today.

_____ 12. Jasper Johnson and his many friends are down-home folks just like you. Jasper uses Sunshine Car Polish, and it makes his car glow. Why don't you go out and buy some Sunshine Car Polish today!

_____ 13. Do you feel depressed and out of energy? Would you like to feel like Tarzan? Then buy and try our new Jungle Vitamins and load up your body with life.

_____ 14. Use Fatso Shampoo and make your hair more resilient and more dynamic. Fatso is organically formulated and uses the metabolic elements that your hair demands.

_____ 15. All dogs who eat Gloopy Dog Food will bark for joy when you fill their bowls with Gloopy Dog Food.

PATTERNS OF ERRORS

_____ Inability to detect and interpret propaganda techniques

LEVEL R

Number possible __15__

Number correct _____

Accuracy _____

COMMENTS: _____

_____

ANSWER KEY FOR THE COMPREHENSION SKILLS INVENTORIES

LEVEL A

1. D	6. C	11. B	16. D	21. C
2. A	7. B	12. C	17. A	22. A
3. E	8. D	13. E	18. E	23. E
4. B	9. A	14. A	19. B	24. B
5. C	10. E	15. D	20. C	25. D

NOTE: The words contained in this level were randomly selected from a set of basal readers. If you want to make the test more personalized, select words from your reading lessons and substitute them for the words used here.

LEVEL B

1. B	3. C	5. A	7. C	9. B
2. A	4. B	6. A	8. A	10. A

LEVEL C

1. B	3. B	5. C	7. B	9. A
2. A	4. A	6. A	8. C	10. B

LEVEL D

1. A	1. B	1. B
2. C	2. B	2. B
3. B	3. C	3. C
	4. A	

LEVEL E

The mystery word is DIRECTIONS.

Row 1: snowmobile, truck
Row 2: taco, peanuts
Row 3: apron, scarf
Row 4: ball, doll
Row 5: dish, knife

LEVEL F

1. 8, 10, 12	Sequence: <u>2</u>
2. DDDD	<u>3</u>
3. TAP	<u>1</u>
4. 8 + 13	<u>5</u>
5. DW	<u>4</u>

LEVEL G

A.	1. B	B.	1. C	C.	1. B
	2. C		2. B		2. C
	3. C		3. A		3. B
			4. B		

LEVEL H

1. G	3. K	5. F	7. N	9. C
2. L	4. D	6. H	8. J	10. B

LEVEL I

1. A	3. C	5. C	7. B	9. B
2. B	4. A	6. B	8. C	10. B

LEVEL J

Answers may vary.
A. 1. Roads were flooded.
   2. Homes were destroyed by the flood waters.
   3. Stores were flooded and had to close to business.

B. 1. food   3. a weapon
   2. drinking water   4. extra clothing

C. 1. Find a security guard.
   2. Try to retrace her steps to her mother.
   3. Go to the nearest clerk and ask for help.

LEVEL K

A.	1. B	B.	1. B	C.	1. C & D
	2. B		2. A		2. A & C
	3. B		3. A		

LEVEL L

1. E	3. A	5. I	7. G	9. J
2. B	4. F	6. H	8. D	10. C

LEVEL M

List 1	3	List 2	5	List 3	2	List 4	1
	5		3		4		5
	1		4		1		2
	2		2		5		4
	4		1		3		3

LEVEL N

SOCIAL STUDIES	SCIENCE	ARITHMETIC	ENGLISH
latitude	biology	addend	sentence
explore	Uranus	tens	paragraph
climate	molecules	equals	adverb
irrigation	orbit	column	capitalization
disaster	experiment	addition	punctuate

LEVEL O

1. C	6. I	1. because
2. G	7. F	2. Because
3. J	8. B	3. for this reason
4. H	9. A	4. and consequently
5. E	10. D	5. therefore

LEVEL P (PART I)

1. D
2. B
3. C
4. E
5. A

LEVEL P (PART II)

1. C
2. B
3. C
4. C
5. B

LEVEL Q

1. B	1. B	6. C
2. E	2. A	7. A
3. C	3. C	8. C
4. A	4. A	9. B
5. D	5. B	10. A

LEVEL R

1. A	4. E	7. B	10. D	13. F
2. D	5. B	8. C	11. C	14. D
3. C	6. F	9. A	12. E	15. B

INFORMAL SURVIVAL READING SKILLS INVENTORIES

TEACHER'S GUIDE

Introduction

The following informal reading inventories have been designed to diagnose reading problems in the area of survival reading skills. To assess areas of deficiency, it is necessary for students to complete <u>all</u> sections of the inventories. Deficiencies in any of the areas should be recorded on the Survival Reading Skills Checklist on page 97. The inventories are designed for students in grades four and up.

Directions

The following are general directions for administering the informal reading inventories for survival reading skills.

1. Explain to the student that he or she is expected to complete <u>all</u> test sections. Be certain that each child understands what he or she is expected to do on each test section.
2. As you administer the test, write on an index card comments about any problems you may observe.
3. Give the student a rest period when needed.

Scoring

Refer to the Answer Key on pages 111-112 for answers to the exercises. Students should be able to answer test items with 100% accuracy. Any incorrect answers indicate an area of deficiency.

Checklist

1. On the Survival Reading Skills Checklist, place a check mark next to the student's area(s) of deficiency as indicated by incorrect answers on the test.
2. Record any additional comments in the space provided.

Checklist of Specific Skill Weaknesses

Survival Reading Skills

NAME _____ GRADE __ TEACHER _____

DATE _____ SCHOOL _____

_____ I.   Interpreting and completing forms

_____ II. Interpreting product information

_____ III. Following directions

_____ IV. Locating and using references

       _____ Using the table of contents to locate information

       _____ Interpreting information found in the card catalog

       _____ Using information found in a dictionary

       _____ Utilizing information found in an index

       _____ Finding information in an encyclopedia

       _____ Interpreting information found in the <u>Readers' Guide to Periodical Literature</u>

       _____ Interpreting information found on a map

Survival Reading Skills

NAME _____ GRADE __ TEACHER _____

DATE _____ SCHOOL _____

I. Interpreting and Completing Forms

Directions: When you want to receive a particular magazine on a regular basis, you may save money by subscribing to that magazine. Read the following subscription information and then answer the questions.

High Adventure Magazine

Please send me a one-year subscription to High Adventure magazine. I understand that I will be billed at the special introductory rate of $3.95 (including postage and handling). The special introductory price is for a one-year subscription and is $1.00 less than the regular yearly subscription rate.

Questions: 1. When compared to the regular yearly subscription rate, will you save money by applying for this special introductory offer?

_____ If so, how much? _____

2. If you already subscribe to High Adventure magazine, can you renew your subscription for $3.95? _____ Why or why not?

_____

_____

3. If you order this magazine, will your total bill be exactly $3.95?

_____ How do you know? _____

_____

Survival Reading Skills

NAME _____ GRADE __ TEACHER _____

DATE _____ SCHOOL _____

II. A. Interpreting Product Information

Directions: Before using a particular product, you should always read and study the information on the label. Read the product label below and then answer the questions.

Dorsol Crawling Insect Spray

Dorsol Crawling Insect Spray kills roaches, ants, silverfish, centipedes, spiders, and most other crawling insects.

Directions for Use: Spray all surfaces that insects crawl over: doorways, walks, window ledges, etc. Do not spray on children's toys or in areas where pets will be playing. Caution should be exercised in using this product; it is very toxic.

Questions: 1. What type of insects will be killed by this spray?

_____

2. What does the word <u>toxic</u> mean? _____

3. Will this spray kill mosquitoes? _____ Why or why not?

_____

Survival Reading Skills

NAME _____ GRADE __ TEACHER _____

DATE _____ SCHOOL _____

II. B. Interpreting Product Information

Directions: You can determine the nutritional value of the food products you purchase by reading the product labels. Read the label information below and then answer the questions.

© 1985 by Parker Publishing Company, Inc.

Yummy Yogurt—Nutrition Information Per Serving

Serving Size .... 10 oz.

Servings Per Container 2

Calories 190

Percentages of U.S. Recommended Daily Allowances
(U.S. RDA)

Protein 20

Vitamin A .... *

Vitamin B 12 15

Thiamine 10

Vitamin C .... *

*Contains less than 2% of the U.S. RDA
of these nutrients.

Distributed by: The YOTO Food Processing Company
Pittsburgh, PA

Questions: 1. If two people were served equal portions from this container of yogurt, how many ounces would each person receive? _____

2. This product contains less than 2% of the U.S. RDA of what substances? _____

3. If you wanted to communicate with a representative of the company, where would you send your letter? _____

_____

Survival Reading Skills

NAME _____ GRADE __ TEACHER _____

DATE _____ SCHOOL _____

III. A. Following Directions

Directions: Before operating a kitchen appliance, you should read the directions for the use and care of the appliance. Read the following information regarding the use of a popcorn popper and then answer the questions.

Popcorn Popper Directions

This popcorn popper is designed for trouble-free operation. However, under certain circumstances, a thermostat in the unit will shut off the appliance to prevent it from becoming overheated. The following operating conditions may cause the thermostat to shut off the appliance:

1. Popping for extended periods of time without allowing the popper to cool down.

2. Overfilling the popper with unpopped corn.

3. Operating another appliance along with the popper from the same electrical outlet. This could overload the circuit and cause an electrical overload or a "blown" fuse.

Should the popper stop running, turn the switch to Off and allow the appliance to cool down for 15 to 20 minutes before you attempt to pop any more corn.

Questions: 1. Under certain conditions, what part in the popper will automatically shut off the appliance to prevent overheating?

_____

2. If the popper stops running, what should you do? _____

_____

3. What three conditions can cause the popper to stop running?

_____

_____

_____

Survival Reading Skills

III. B. Following Directions

Directions: Before you operate any piece of equipment, you should be thoroughly familiar with the directions for its use. Read the following directions for the use of a lawn trimmer and then answer the questions.

Lawn Trimmer Directions

This lawn trimmer can save you time and energy and help you keep your lawn looking well trimmed. To assure maximum efficiency and safety in its operation, follow a few simple steps:

1. Always wear goggles or other suitable eye protectors.

2. Never use the trimmer during or immediately after a rain shower.

3. Do not wear jewelry or loose-fitting clothing while you operate the trimmer.

4. Always be sure of your footing before you start the trimmer.

5. If the trimmer should begin to vibrate uncontrollably, turn it off.

Questions: 1. What specific part of your body should you protect when you use the trimmer? _____

2. What type of clothing should you wear when you are using the trimmer? _____

3. How will the trimmer act when it is malfunctioning?

_____

Survival Reading Skills

NAME _____ GRADE __ TEACHER _____

DATE _____ SCHOOL _____

IV. A. Locating and Using References:

Table of Contents

Directions: A table of contents is included in the front of a book or magazine to help you locate information. Study the following sample table of contents and then answer the questions.

Table of Contents

The Big Fisherman   Vol. 20, No. 3   May 1985

Finding the Big Ones 1

The Proper Bait 10

Fishing Conditions 13

South American Fishing 17

Care of the Rod and Reel 19

Questions: 1. On what pages would you find information about fishing in Brazil? _____

2. Which article is the longest? _____

3. If you had a problem with your fishing reel, on what page would you look for information about it? _____

Survival Reading Skills

NAME _____ GRADE __ TEACHER _____

DATE _____ SCHOOL _____

IV. B. Locating and Using References:

The Card Catalog

Directions: When you are trying to locate a book in the library, the card catalog is the first place to check. Each fiction book in the library will have an author card and a title card in the card catalog. Each nonfiction book will have an author card, a title card, and subject heading cards. Study the sample card catalog entries below and then answer the questions.

Card Catalog Entries

CATS

FOOTBALL

Scar, Robert

Treasure Island

Palmer, Richard

Questions: 1. Of the five headings listed above, which are subject headings? _____

2. Treasure Island is what type of card catalog entry?

_____

3. List the two author entries.

_____

_____

Survival Reading Skills

NAME _____ GRADE __ TEACHER _____

DATE _____ SCHOOL _____

IV. C. Locating and Using References:

Dictionary

Directions: When you are using a dictionary, the guide words at the top of the pages will help you locate the word you are seeking. Study the following guide words and the entry words that follow. After you have studied the words, complete the exercise.

Guide Words

gin—girl

homerun—homogenize

military—milk

Dictionary Entry Words

milieu	homicide	gipsy
homesick	militia	gingham
ginger	gird	homespun

Dictionary Exercise

Write the dictionary entry words in alphabetical order under the guide words where they would be found in a dictionary.

gin—girl   military—milk

1. _____   1. _____

2. _____   2. _____

3. _____

4. _____

homerun—homogenize

1. _____

2. _____

3. _____

Survival Reading Skills

NAME _____ GRADE ___ TEACHER _____

DATE _____ SCHOOL _____

IV. D. Locating and Using References:
The Index—Part I

Indexing

Directions: Magazines, newspapers, books, and other printed sources often have an index. Read the information contained in the following newspaper index and answer the questions.

Newspaper Index	Pages
Antiques	E 6
Building News	G 2
Fashions	E 4
Food News	E 7-8
Garden News	E 24
Heat and Energy	E 6
Living Today	E 1-5
Movies	F 1-4
Music and Records	F 5-6
People in the News	A 6
Press Chef	E 8
Real Estate	G 3-11
Sports News	D 1-12
Travel and Resorts	F 7-11
Want Ads	C 3-29
Weather Map	A 19

Questions: 1. What are the names of the sections of the newspaper where you would find information on cooking and recipes?

_____

2. If you or someone in your family were looking for a job, under what section of the newspaper would you look?

_____

3. Which section of the newspaper would give the name of the record that is number one on the charts?

_____

4. Which section of the newspaper is the longest?

_____

Survival Reading Skills

NAME _____ GRADE __ TEACHER _____

DATE _____ SCHOOL _____

IV. D. Locating and Using References:

The Index—Part II
Cross-Indexing
Directions: To find information in some indexes, you have to use cross-indexing. Study the questions below and refer to the sample index to find the correct answers.

INDEX

Backpacking Equip & Supplies–see
    Camping Equipment & Supplies 176
    Mountain Climbing Equip 499
Bacteriological Laboratories–see
    Laboratories–Medical 450
Badges–see
    Buttons–Advertising 174
Bagels 125
Baggage Transfer–see
    Express & Transfer Service 288
Bags–Sleeping–see
    Camping Equipment & Supplies 176
Bail Bonds 125
Bait–see
    Fishing Bait 306
Bakers–Retail 125
Ballet Instruction–see
    Dancing Instruction 233
Balloons–see
    Balloons–Manned 127
    Balloons–Novelty & Toy 127
Balloons Gift Delivery–see
    Balloons–Novelty & Toy 127
Balloons–Manned 127
Balloons–Novelty & Toy 127
Ballroom Dancing Instruction–see
    Dancing Instruction 233
Ballrooms 127
Band Instruments–see
    Musical Instruments–Dealers 519
    Musical Instruments–Repairing 522
Band Saws–see
    Saws 691

Questions: 1. On what page would you look to find information about mountain climbing equipment?

         _____

    2. On what page would you look if you wanted to have your trumpet repaired?

         _____

    3. If you were planning to go fishing, what page would give you information about purchasing fishing worms?

         _____

Survival Reading Skills

NAME _____ GRADE __ TEACHER _____

DATE _____ SCHOOL _____

IV. E. Locating and Using References:

Encyclopedia

An encyclopedia is a comprehensive reference source. Information about persons, places, events, and facts of interest and importance are included in an encyclopedia.

Encyclopedia Exercise:

Which of the following questions might be answered in an encyclopedia? Answer YES or NO for each question.

1. What was the most popular sports program on television in 1960?

_____

2. What is an atom? _____

3. How does a motor operate? _____

4. What two teams played in Super Bowl II? _____

Survival Reading Skills

IV. F. Locating and Using References:

The <u>Readers' Guide to Periodical Literature</u>

Directions: If you were doing a report on a current subject, you would need to look up recent magazine articles. An index that can help you locate magazine articles is the <u>Readers' Guide to Periodical Literature</u>. Study the following sample entries from the <u>Readers' Guide</u> and answer the questions.

Sample Entries from the <u>Readers' Guide to Periodical Literature</u>

Earthworms

Selling Worms for Profit. il Nat Sci World 40:20-1 Je'79
Information About Earthworms. il Nat Sci 21:57-62 Jl'79

Questions: 1. What magazine contains an article entitled "Information About Earthworms"? _____

2. In the articles listed above, which months are abbreviated? _____

3. On what pages in <u>National Science World</u> would you find information about earthworms? _____

Survival Reading Skills

NAME _____ GRADE __ TEACHER _____

DATE _____ SCHOOL _____

IV. G. Locating and Using References

Map

Directions: When you travel in an unfamiliar part of the country, you have to read a map to locate the correct route to your destination. Study the map below and then answer the questions.

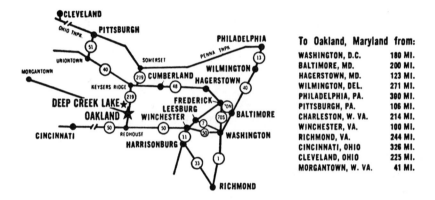

To Oakland, Maryland from:

WASHINGTON, D.C.	180 MI.
BALTIMORE, MD.	200 MI.
HAGERSTOWN, MD.	123 MI.
WILMINGTON, DEL.	271 MI.
PHILADELPHIA, PA.	300 MI.
PITTSBURGH, PA.	106 MI.
CHARLESTON, W. VA.	214 MI.
WINCHESTER, VA.	100 MI.
RICHMOND, VA.	244 MI.
CINCINNATI, OHIO	326 MI.
CLEVELAND, OHIO	225 MI.
MORGANTOWN, W. VA.	41 MI.

Questions: 1. If you lived in Baltimore, Maryland and followed Routes 40 and 13 to Philadelphia, Pennsylvania, what direction according to the compass would you be traveling?

_____

2. What city is the farthest north on this map?

_____

3. How many miles is Oakland, Maryland from Pittsburgh, Pennsylvania?

_____

ANSWER KEY FOR THE SURVIVAL READING SKILLS INVENTORIES

I. 1. Yes. $1.00
    2. No. It is a special introductory offer; therefore, only people who do not already subscribe to the magazine can receive this rate.
    3. Yes. Postage and handling are included in the price.

II. A. 1. Crawling insects
       2. Poisonous
       3. No. Mosquitoes are flying, not crawling insects.

    B. 1. Five ounces
       2. Vitamin A and Vitamin C
       3. To the YOTO Food Processing Company, Pittsburgh, PA.

III. A. 1. Thermostat
        2. Turn switch to Off and allow the appliance to cool down for 15 to 20 minutes.
        3. (a.) Operating the unit for extended periods of time.
           (b.) Overfilling popper with unpopped corn.
           (c.) Operating another appliance from the same electrical outlet.

     B. 1. Eyes
        2. Close-fitting
        3. Vibrate

IV. A. 1. Pages 17 and 18
       2. Finding the Big Ones
       3. Page 19

    B. 1. CATS and FOOTBALL
       2. Title
       3. Scar, Robert and Palmer, Richard

    C. 1. ginger   1. homesick   1. milieu
       2. gingham   2. homespun   2. militia
       3. gipsy   3. homicide
       4. gird

    D. (1) 1. Food News and Press Chef   (2) 1. 499
           2. Want Ads   2. 522
           3. Music and Records   3. 306
           4. Want Ads

E. 1. No
   2. Yes
   3. Yes
   4. No

F. 1. <u>Natural Science</u>
   2. June and July
   3. Pages 20 to 21 in the June 1979 issue

G. 1. North
   2. Cleveland
   3. 106

Section 2

INDIVIDUAL
PUPIL CHECKLIST
OF READING SKILLS

Checklists are helpful in tabulating the patterns of problems that are characteristic of disabled readers. The "Individual Pupil Checklist of Reading Skills," which specifically identifies areas of reading weakness, should be used when you are trying to identify and remediate areas of specific reading deficiencies. It should be completed after you have administered the informal reading inventories. Because of its extensive listing of problem areas, you will find this checklist to be an invaluable diagnostic instrument.

The checklist is designed to aid you in recording diagnosed areas of reading deficiency. In order for the checklist to be of value, you will need to reevaluate the pupil's needs and update the checklist frequently. The checklist contains four error categories that are divided into skill areas:

1. Word Recognition Skills
   a. Phonetic analysis
   b. Structural analysis

2. Comprehension Skills
   a. Vocabulary
   b. Literal comprehension
   c. Interpretive comprehension
   d. Critical reading

3. Oral Reading Skills

4. Survival Reading Skills

As you know from your own teaching experience, these four areas are of major importance. To complete and use the checklist, place a check mark beside the skills that are known, leave the weak skills blank, and place an X in the blank beside the skills that have not been assessed. As the child improves in the weak skill areas and/or the unassessed skills are evaluated, the appropriate recordkeeping marks are placed in the blanks.

Reading deficiencies identified on the checklist are the areas to be remediated. The remediation activities contained in *Classroom Activities for Correcting Specific Reading Problems*, also available from the publisher, are keyed to the skill areas as listed on the "Individual Pupil Checklist of Reading Skills." The checklist as presented here is designed to be completed for each student in your classroom. By using the checklist and the remediation activities in the companion volume, you can plan effective and interesting lessons that will remediate the student's areas of deficiency.

INDIVIDUAL PUPIL CHECKLIST OF READING SKILLS

NAME: _____ GRADE: ____ TEACHER: _____

Directions: Place a check mark beside each skill the child knows, leave the space blank if the child does not know the skill, and place an X beside each skill that has not been assessed.

I. Word Recognition Skills
  A. Letter Recognition
    1. Recognizes upper case letters _____
    2. Recognizes lower case letters _____
    3. Reverses letters _____
    4. Inverts letters _____
    5. Recognizes letters in the initial position _____
    6. Recognizes letters in the medial position _____
    7. Recognizes letters in the final position _____
  B. Letter Sound Recognition
    1. Identifies rhymes in words _____
    2. Identifies word family rhymes _____
    3. Recognizes and names consonant sounds _____
    4. Recognizes and names vowel sounds _____
  C. Consonant Recognition
    1. Recognizes initial consonants _____
    2. Recognizes final consonants _____
    3. Recognizes initial two-letter blends _____
    4. Recognizes initial three-letter blends _____
    5. Recognizes final consonant blends _____
    6. Recognizes initial consonant digraphs _____
    7. Recognizes final consonant digraphs _____
    8. Recognizes "y" as a consonant _____
    9. Recognizes consonant irregularities
      a. Two sounds of **c** _____
      b. Two sounds of **g** _____
      c. **s** as **s, z,** and **sh** _____
  D. Vowel Recognition
    1. Recognizes long vowel sounds _____
    2. Recognizes short vowel sounds _____
    3. Recognizes schwa sounds _____
    4. Recognizes vowel digraphs _____
    5. Recognizes vowel diphthongs _____
    6. Understands vowel rules
      a. CVC _____
      b. CVCe _____
      c. CVVC _____
      d. CV _____

7. Understands vowel rule exceptions
   a. **o** followed by **ld** and **lt** ____
   b. **a** followed by **l, ll, w,** and **u** ____
   c. **i** followed by **nd, gh,** and **ld** ____
   d. vowel followed by **r** ____
   e. **y** as a vowel ____
E. Word Analysis (Structural Analysis)
   1. Can identify compound words ____
   2. Can identify inflectional endings ____
   3. Can identify root words ____
   4. Can identify contractions ____
   5. Can identify possessives ____
   6. Can identify plurals
      a. **s** ____
      b. **es** ____
      c. **ies** ____
      d. **ves** ____
      e. **y** endings ____
F. Syllabication (Structural Analysis)
   1. Can divide words into syllables
      a. one-syllable words ____
      b. two-syllable words ____
      c. three-syllable words ____
      d. four-syllable words ____
      e. five- and six-syllable words ____
   2. Can apply syllabication rules
      a. VCV ____
      b. VCCV ____
      c. -le ____
      d. single vowel as a syllable ____
      e. consonant blends and digraphs ____
      f. prefixes and suffixes ____
II. Comprehension Skills
   A. Vocabulary
      1. Understands words in isolation ____
      2. Understands multiple meaning words in context ____
      3. Understands technical words in context ____
   B. Literal Comprehension
      1. Recalls facts read ____
      2. Follows directions read ____
      3. Sequences ideas read ____
      4. Selects important details ____

C. Interpretive Reading Skills
   1. Can identify main ideas not explicitly stated   ____
   2. Can draw logical conclusions   ____
   3. Can predict logical outcomes   ____
   4. Can interpret key concepts about story characters   ____
   5. Can associate the text with the correct picture   ____
   6. Can follow plot sequence   ____
   7. Can classify information   ____
   8. Can determine cause-and-effect relationships   ____
   9. Can summarize material read   ____

D. Critical Reading Skills
   1. Can identify and understand figures of speech (similes, metaphors, personification, etc.)   ____
   2. Can detect and interpret propaganda techniques (testimonials, glittering generalities, bandwagon, etc.)   ____

III. Oral Reading Skills

Before completing the items in this section, administer an informal reading inventory or an oral reading test to the pupil. Use the diagnostic information obtained from the test to complete this section.

  A. Pronounces words correctly   ____
  B. Uses appropriate voice intonation, pitch, and stress   ____
  C. Uses punctuation marks correctly during oral reading   ____
  D. Reads in correct phrases   ____
  E. Reads with clear and distinct enunciation and appropriate expression   ____
  F. Uses appropriate eye-voice span   ____

IV. Survival Reading Skills
  A. Can interpret and complete forms   ____
  B. Can interpret product information   ____
  C. Can follow directions   ____
  D. Can locate and use references
    1. Can use the table of contents to locate information   ____
    2. Can interpret information found in the card catalog   ____
    3. Can use information found in a dictionary   ____
    4. Can use information found in an index   ____
    5. Can find information in an encyclopedia   ____
    6. Can interpret information found in the Readers' Guide to Periodical Literature   ____
    7. Can interpret information found on a map   ____

Section 3

INTERVIEW FORMS

The following Child Interview Form and Parent Interview Form help you to understand the needs of the child.

The questions on the Child Interview Form are designed to provide you with information about the child's family, home environment, school activities, hobbies, study habits, and after-school activities. Answers to the questions provide information that can be used to analyze or remediate reading deficiencies. Although the intermediate grade child could read the information contained on the questionnaire, you should ask the questions orally and encourage the child to discuss the answers in detail. The same procedure should also be used for the primary grade child.

The Parent Interview Form should be completed during a parent conference. The questions on the form are designed to explore the child's home life, medical problems, reading environment, and parents' attitude toward the child's reading problem. To obtain an understanding of factors that may be hindering the child's reading progress, compare the responses on the Parent Interview Form with the responses on the Child Interview Form. Different answers to similar questions on the two forms will need to be explored further.

CHILD INTERVIEW FORM

Child's Name _____   Name of School attended _____

Grade Level _____   Phone Number of School _____

School's Address _____   Teacher's Name _____

Child's Birthdate _____   Child's Address _____

Child's Home Phone Number _____   Chronological Age _____

Mental Age _____

Parent's Name _____   Interviewer's Name _____

1. With whom do you like to play at school? _____
2. With whom do you like to play at home? _____
3. What games do you play with your friends? _____
4. What do you do when you come home from school? _____
5. Do you have any brothers or sisters? _____
   a. What are their names? _____
   b. How old are they? _____
   c. Do they like to play with you? _____
6. What is your father's name? _____
   a. What kind of work does he do? _____
   b. What games does he play with you? _____
   c. What books do you read together? _____
7. What is your mother's name? _____
   a. What kind of work does she do? _____
   b. If she works, who watches you when she is at work? _____
   c. What games does she play with you? _____
   d. What books do you read together? _____
8. Do you go to the community library? _____
   a. How often? _____
9. Do you go to the school library? _____
   a. How often? _____
10. What library books are you presently reading? _____
11. What library books have you read this year? _____
12. Do you belong to any clubs? _____
    a. Which ones? _____
    b. Why did you join? _____
13. Do you have a hobby? _____
    a. What is it? _____
    b. Why do you like this hobby? _____
14. Do you take any special lessons? _____
    a. What? _____
    b. Why do you take the lessons? _____
15. What are your favorite television programs? _____
    a. How often do you watch television? _____
    b. Do you do your homework while you watch television? _____

16. Where do you do your homework? _____
    a. When do you do your homework? _____
    b. Who helps you with your homework? _____
    c. Do you like that person to help you? _____
17. What are your favorite radio programs? _____
    a. Do you do your homework while you listen to the radio? _____
18. Do you have a pet? _____
    a. What kind of pet? _____
    b. Where did you get it? _____
    c. Why did you get it? _____
    d. Do you take care of it? _____
19. Have you gone to any other schools? _____
    a. Where? _____
    b. How many? _____
    c. Do you like the school you are now attending? _____
    d. Why do you or don't you like the school? _____

PARENT INTERVIEW FORM

Pupil's Name _____ Parents' Names _____
Father's Approximate Age _____ Educated to Grade _____
Mother's Approximate Age _____ Educated to Grade _____
Parents are: Living Together _____, Separated _____, Divorced _____,
Deceased (either or both) _____. Name of the child's guardian if
the child isn't living with parents: _____

1. Are any foreign languages spoken in the home? _____
   a. Which ones? _____
   b. By whom? _____
2. Are any grandparents living in the home? _____
   a. Maternal or paternal grandparents? _____
3. Does the child have any health problems? _____
   a. What are they? _____
4. Does the child require any special medicine? _____
   a. What? _____
   b. How often? _____
   c. Why? _____
5. Is the child allergic to anything? _____
   a. What? _____
   b. How does it affect the child? _____
6. Does the child have any speech problems? _____
   a. What? _____
   b. Does the child go to a speech therapist? _____
      1. How often? _____
7. Does the child have any vision problems? _____
   a. Does the child wear glasses? _____
8. Does the child have any hearing problems? _____
   a. Does the child wear a hearing aid? _____
9. Did the child have any special problems as a baby? _____
   a. What? _____
   b. When? _____
   c. What was done for the child to cure the problem? _____
10. What previous tutoring has the child had? _____
    a. When? _____
    b. By whom? _____
    c. For what? _____
    d. Did it help the child? _____
11. What reading materials are in the home? _____
    a. Books _____
    b. Magazines _____
    c. Newspapers _____
    d. Children's Books _____

12. Does anyone read to the child at home? _____
    a. Who? _____
    b. When? _____
    c. What books? _____
13. What does the parent see as the child's most severe reading problem(s)? ___
_____
14. What does the parent see as the child's academic strengths? _____
_____
15. What does the parent see as the child's academic weaknesses? _____
_____
16. Other remarks: _____
_____

Section 4

INTEREST INVENTORIES

Knowledge of the students' major areas of interest will help you select appropriate instructional exercises. Research has shown that students read interesting material more easily and with higher comprehension. The interest inventory is an informal projective test that encourages the student to react to the open-ended questions in a nonrestrictive manner. Depending upon the pupil's reading ability, either he or she reads the interest inventory independently, or you read the questions to the child. In either situation, the main purpose for the inventory is to identify the pupil's area(s) of higher interest. Questions on the interest inventory investigate the pupil's experiential background, his or her reading patterns, books and magazines read, and his or her other interests. By administering the interest inventory and analyzing the results, you will gain insight into areas of high interest that can be used in the reading lessons. Lessons planned for the child should be centered around his or her areas of highest interest.

On the following pages you will find two interest inventories—one for the primary-level child and one for the intermediate-level child. By selecting and administering the inventory that is appropriate for the children in your classroom, you will be gathering information that will help you create lessons that are of high interest to your students. As we all know, if a child is interested in the material, he or she will be more willing to complete the lesson.

Interest Inventory (Primary Grade Level)
Oral or Written Form

NAME _____ GRADE ____ TEACHER _____ DATE _____

1. What are the names of your three favorite television programs?

2. What do you like to do with your father?

3. What do you like to do with your mother?

4. What do you like to do with your brother and/or sister?

5. What is your favorite place to visit? Why?

6. What is the title of your favorite book that somone has read to you?

7. What is the title of your favorite book that you have read yourself?

8. Have you ever been to the library?

9. Have you ever attended a story hour at the library?

10. What are the titles of some of the books you have at home?

11. Do you read the comics in the Sunday paper?

12. What is the name of your favorite comic character?

13. What is the name of your favorite television character?

14. What are the names of your favorite games to play?

15. What toys or playthings, that you have at home, are your favorites?

16. Is there any toy or plaything you especially want? What is it?

17. Who are your best friends?

18. How often do you play with your friends?

19. What things do you enjoy doing with your friends?

20. Have you ever been to these places? (Circle the ones that the child has **been** to.)

a farm	a department store	a planetarium
a zoo	the beach	a theater
a parade	an amusement park	a museum
a circus	a store	the mountains

21. If you had three wishes that might come true, what would you wish for?

22. If you could be anybody else in the world, whom would you want to be? Why?

Interest Inventory (Intermediate Grade Level)
Written Form

NAME _____ GRADE ____ TEACHER _____ DATE _____

1. What are the names of your four favorite television programs?

2. What television sports programs are your favorites?

3. Do you make collections of things? What are they?

4. What clubs or organizations do you belong to?

5. What school subjects do you like?

6. What school subjects are of least interest to you?

7. What books have you read in the last two months?

8. What is the title of the most interesting book you ever read?

9. What magazines do you get at home?

10. Do you read the newspaper? Which parts of the paper do you read?

11. Do you go to the library?

12. Do you have a library card?

13. Who are your best friends?

14. What do you enjoy doing with your friends?

15. What do you enjoy doing with your father?

16. What do you enjoy doing with your mother?

17. What do you enjoy doing with your brother and/or sister?

18. What types of books do you like best?
travel	sports	mystery
science	adventure	biographies

19. Does anyone help you discover and select books that you might enjoy? Who?

20. Do you play a musical instrument? Which one? For how long have you played it?

21. Do you have a job through which you earn money during the week or on Saturdays?

22. What places have you visited in your state?

23. What places have you visited in other states or countries?

Section 5

ATTITUDE
SURVEYS

Along with interest inventories, attitude surveys are an important part of a diagnostic program. The attitude survey identifies the pupil's attitude toward various areas such as self, home, parents, school, reading, and peers. Questions on the attitude survey are designed as incomplete sentences that permit the pupil to answer the questions in a nonrestrictive manner. To avoid grouping the areas to be explored into separate sections, the questions are rotated in patterns of five. Questions 1, 6, 11, 16, etc., for example, explore one attitude area, and questions 2, 7, 12, 17, etc. explore another attitude area. In analyzing the survey, you study each group of questions that relate to the specified attitude area. Results of the survey are used to analyze affective areas that may be interfering with reading progress.

On the following pages you will find surveys that are administered to the primary- or the intermediate-level child. By administering the appropriate survey, you will acquire information on the child that will increase your ability to meet his or her individual needs. By using the results of an attitude survey, you can evaluate how the child feels about his or her reading ability. If on an initial survey the child feels he or she is reading poorly, you can work to improve the child's self-concept. Because of your work, the end-of-the-year survey may reveal that the child now believes he or she is a good reader.

Incomplete Sentences Test (Primary Grade Level)

NAME _____ GRADE ____ TEACHER _____ DATE _____

Directions: Complete the following sentences to express how you really feel. There are no right or wrong answers.

1. Today I will _____
2. My father is _____
3. Reading is _____
4. Classes are _____
5. My friends are _____
6. I hope I will _____
7. People are _____
8. Words are _____
9. For me, homework _____
10. I like to play with _____
11. In the evening I _____
12. My mother is _____
13. Special help in reading is _____
14. In school I _____
15. Playing games is _____
16. I like to _____
17. My brother and/or sister _____
18. Comic books are _____
19. I read better than _____
20. If my friends would _____
21. I feel good when _____
22. I wish my father would _____
23. I'd like reading more if _____
24. Recess is _____
25. My friend is _____
26. I wish that _____
27. I think my mother _____

131

28. Studying is _____

29. Teachers are _____

30. I get unhappy when _____

31. People think I _____

32. Most brothers and sisters _____

33. I like to study when _____

34. Reading science _____

35. I wish people would _____

36. I often worry about _____

37. My grandparents are _____

38. Reading class is _____

39. My favorite subject in school is _____

40. I hope to be _____

41. I work best when _____

42. My mother says _____

43. The last book I read was _____

44. Reading history is _____

45. Hobbies are _____

46. I want to _____

47. My family _____

48. Magazines are _____

49. I'd enjoy school more if _____

50. All children should _____

Incomplete Sentences Test (Intermediate Grade Level)

NAME _____GRADE ____ TEACHER _____DATE _____

Directions: Complete the following sentences to express how you really feel. There are no right or wrong answers.

1. Today I will _____

2. I wish that my father _____

3. Reading is _____

4. I think that school is _____

5. Friends are _____

6. It is easy for me to _____

7. I wish that my mother _____

8. The thing I like best about reading _____

9. My teachers are _____

10. My favorite person is _____

11. I am afraid that _____

12. My brother and/or sister _____

13. History books are _____

14. Homework is _____

15. My friends always _____

16. I wish I could _____

17. I like it when my father _____

18. Comic books are _____

19. My best subject is _____

20. People think I _____

21. It is difficult for me to _____

22. My mother _____

23. Sometimes the words in books _____

24. On the way home from school _____

25. My best friend _____

26. I get ashamed when _____

27. My family _____

28. Books are _____

29. I think most teachers _____

30. You need friends to _____

31. I feel good when _____

32. My brother/sister is _____

33. The hardest thing about reading is _____

34. One thing I don't like about school is _____

35. My favorite game is _____